Jewelry Designs with
Knitted Wire

Explore the possibilities

Nealay Patel

KALMBACH BOOKS

WAUKESHA, WI

Kalmbach Books
21027 Crossroads Circle
Waukesha, Wisconsin 53186
www.JewelryAndBeadingStore.com

Published in 2015
19 18 17 16 15   1 2 3 4 5

Manufactured in the United States of America

ISBN: 978-1-62700-235-6
EISBN: 978-1-62700-236-3

Editor: Erica Swanson
Book Design: Lisa Bergman
Photographer: William Zuback

Library of Congress Control Number: 2015930765

Preface

I think "exploring" was the big idea for this book, but that term has applied in so many areas of my life. I've had many fortunate circumstances in meeting all kinds of people throughout my travels. Whether it was bead shows, television, or working with beading magazines, they've guided and taught me to be a better designer, and more importantly, a better person.

There were areas I wanted to explore while putting this book together, such as new materials and fresh color palettes, but I really had to take a step back to understand just whom I'm writing to. If I had to choose another word to describe my attitude towards this project, it would be organic. I purposely did not sketch too much in order to keep my process very spur-the-moment – I think this kept things interesting. This was very much the opposite approach from my last book, where I practiced a very rigid method to designing my works.

Something I've always been attracted to is bright colors, simply because they make me happy. So I went crazy with using all kinds of seed beads, but the real excitement came from using larger decorative beads and incorporating them into my beadwork. I appreciate the unusual mixture of big, funky, and chunky with delicate beadwork in each design, making this collection a real exploration of design, color, and innovation.

Contents

Projects

Introduction

Exploring the possibilities

A fateful meeting with Nina Kersten from *SilverSilk* introduced me to the wonderful world of knitted wire—and what a world it is! She kindly let me have some samples to play with, which sat around for months, waiting for some creativity. As inspiration hit, I brought out the knitted wire and my head flooded with ideas as I began to add layers of stitching—in, between, aside, and even around the knitted wire. With that, I developed the concept and fashion direction for this book.

From working with the knitted wire, I've learned how to manipulate my materials to create form, shape, and structure, all while mixing my love of bead weaving into the design. There are several lines of knitted wire, including hollow, flat, capture and leather, for a multitude of creative options. In experimenting with each line, I've developed projects that take the best feature, such as passing half-hard wire through the hollow knitted wire, to achieve a unique—and new—technique.

What I enjoy about using knitted wire is the versatility it gives me for making beadwoven projects. I've taken advantage of the knit-holes of the knitted wire to act as a filigree element. The knit holes make it easy to pass a needle through, sometimes multiple times, for stitching beads. This is also great for novice beaders who want to try working with seed beads for the first time.

In continuing my exploration of knitted wire, the best of what I've discovered is that knitted wire doesn't fray when it's trimmed! This is an important feature that allowed for making small beaded components. You'll find a variety of colors and finishes, which, as you'll see, results in a very colorful and intriguing jewelry collection.

Attaching findings can be difficult. One may develop clever ways to secure the ends, and often the process ends up being messy and tedious. Luckily, there is a wide assortment of clasps and end caps, available in different metals, for securing the ends to perfection. I've included a full chapter that encompasses the different findings and techniques used to secure the designs.

Exploration was important in the discovery of new uses for the knitted wire, and in turn it has helped me rediscover myself and propel my evolution as a designer. I became inspired by the current trend in colors and styles, while staying true to mine. What I've developed is a collection of new works that showcase the best of me and the materials I've chosen to use. I hope you will enjoy making each design and wear it proudly.

Basics

TOOL KIT

Nothing is more important than having the right tools for creating quality jewelry. Trust me, I speak from experience! It took me a while to discover which tools are the most useful and easy to use, and I finally invested in a very good set. Listed below are the basic tools that you need to have in your tool kit to complete all of the projects in this book.

Pliers

Crimping pliers are used to secure the crimp tubes to beading wire. The crimp pliers have two notches or compartments, within the pliers for creating a folded crimp. The flat part at the very tip of the pliers may be used to make a flattened crimp.

Chainnose pliers have flat jaws that taper into a narrow point at the tip. These pliers are great for opening and closing jump rings, pulling the beading wire through tight spaces, and picking up small beads and components. I would advise trying to find a pair with narrow tips, because they're more versatile.

Roundnose pliers have round jaws and taper to a narrow tip. These pliers are mostly used for creating simple loops. The size of the loop is determined by the placement of the wire within the jaws of the pliers. For making consistent loops, use a marker to indicate the spot on the pliers' jaws where you want the loop to be made. This way, all your loops will be the same exact size.

Nylon jaw pliers will become your best friend when working with half-hard wire. Just slide a piece of wire through a pair of pliers a few times to straighten the devil out of it. To polish wire, place a jeweler's cloth between the jaws of the pliers before running the wire through them.

Cutters and Scissors

Cutters have tapered blades that come to a sharp point and are used to cut half-hard wire, beading wire or knitted wire. I recommend investing in a great pair of cutters so they won't wear over time and will continue to cut precisely every time you use them.

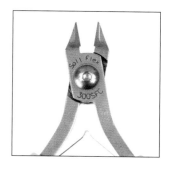 

A small pair of **sharp scissors** dedicated only to trimming beading thread is a great tool to have in your tool kit. It's a good idea not to use these scissors to cut other things like paper or plastic. This will dull the blades quickly and they won't be able to cut thread anymore.

Beading Tools

My favorite needles to use are **size 12 English beading needles**. These needles are 2 in. (5cm) long and are big enough to work with, but thin enough to fit through the tiniest of beads. It's a good idea to have a handful of needles in your tool kit, just in case a needle bends in half or breaks in the middle of a project.

A **bead stopper** is a small clamp, which may be a spring coil or an electrical test clip. Bead stoppers are wonderful for temporarily holding multiple beaded strands or beading thread as you work. You can never have enough bead stoppers, but you may want to start off with two to three in your inventory before going nuts.

A **beading mat** is a soft, felt-like fabric swatch that is used as a place mat for making your beadwork. There are many benefits of working on a beading mat: it will prevent your beads from scratching against a bare table and it will keep them from escaping your workspace. I recommend having at least two or three in your tool kit, so that you have enough workspace to spread out all your beads and have fun.

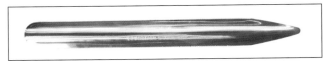

I love my **bead scoop**! There comes a time when my beading table demands to be cleared off. Rather than hand-picking little piles of beads off my table, my handy bead scoop takes care of rounding up those tedious little beads. And the narrow tip is perfect for pouring them back into the narrow tube they came from.

Wireworking Tools

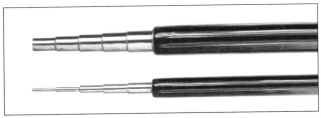

You don't have to buy jump rings when you can make your own. Small handheld **mandrels** are perfect for coiling wire in all kinds of sizes to make jump rings.

I'm no wire expert, but I sure can fool many people with a **jig**. The arrangement, shapes, and sizes of the pegs hold no bounds for the imagination to run wild for making fun and unusual shapes with half-hard wire (I use *Now That's a Jig*™). Combine these handmade wire shapes with the knitted wire, and you've got one stellar jewelry component!

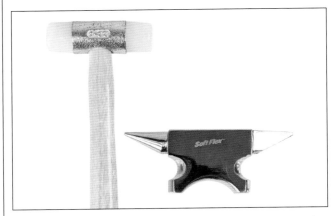

You'll want to have a **hammer and anvil** on hand when working with half-hard wire. These tools will specifically be used for strengthening wire components. The hammer can be fairly small, but it should have a nylon or rubber tip to avoid creating abrasion on the wire.

MATERIALS

Knitted wire is made from 99.9% pure enameled copper wire that is nearly as thin as a human hair. A great feature of knitted wire is that it can be cut without fraying. This makes it easy to use without having to worry about how to secure the ends. Knitted wire is sold in 3 ft. (1m) and 25 ft. (7.6m) spools and comes in an assortment of colors, including a special color called pearlesque, which gives the knitted wire a rainbow-like tint.

There are four types of knitted wires that you'll find when shopping for materials:

Hollow knitted wire is a 3mm round mesh tube with a hollow center. It can be customized by passing 2mm crystals, small seed beads, leather, or silk cord through the center to create your own style.

Capture knitted wire is a small chain of metal beads that fill the hollow space of the knitted wire. This allows easy sewing between the knit-holes while maintaining strength and architecture.

Flat knitted wire is made from an 8-needle stitch, then pressed flat to make a wire, mesh-like ribbon that is 4.8mm wide. It has incredible strength and stiffness and its shape cannot be altered.

Leather knitted wire is made from a six-needle stitch that is carefully woven around 2mm leather cord. The appearance is really unusual with the hard leather and the fine, delicate wire knit that encases it.

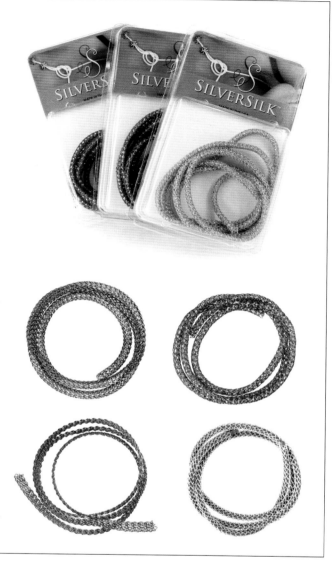

Beads

One of my favorite off-time activities includes going to bead stores or bead shows to indulge in my habit of staring at shiny things... indeed, what else could it be beside beads! There are all kinds of beads out there, and for a novice beader it can be intimidating in choosing the perfect beads, or maybe even the exact beads for a specific project. So in this section, I put together a concise guide that illustrates and describes the beads I used for the projects in this book. Any of these beads should be available in your local bead or hobby store. Do learn all the beads below, but don't be afraid to explore whatever beads may catch your eye!

Drop beads are tear-shaped beads with a hole through the narrow tip at the top of the bead. These Japanese beads are great for creating thick fringe with smooth texture or adding a great pop of color to a design. Drop beads come in a variety of sizes, including a longer oblong shape called a *long drop bead*.

Magatama beads are wide, tear-shaped, and come from Japan. They are wider and broader than the drop beads and come in two sizes: 4mm and 4x7mm (called *long magatama beads*). The long magatama beads are slightly different than regular magatama beads because the holes, and the bead itself, is slanted so that they lean when stitched. I love the texture that both sizes offer when stitched in with other beads.

Cube beads are square-shaped beads with a wide hole. Like seed beads, the size of cube beads is measured in aughts, and comes in many colors and sizes. The mass of each cube bead results in a sturdy beaded foundation when stitched together. The large hole is great if you need to stitch through it several times.

Tila beads are flat, square-shaped beads, measuring 5x5x1.9mm with two parallel holes. Use these beads for weaving flat knitted wire between the beads or even color-blocking when stitching them together.

Tiny glass **seed beads** truly represent the name they are given, because they are miniscule in size, but are a blast to work with! Seed beads are measured in a unit called aught, represented by the symbol $^\circ$. As the size of your seed bead increases, the aught number decreases. The designs in this book use Japanese seed beads because they are uniform, have a wide bead hole, and come in a variety of colors and sizes.

Large **decorative beads** add dimension, depth, and a splash of color to your projects. Decorative beads may be made of glass, fiber, ceramic, handmade, or natural beads and come in a variety of colors, sizes, and textures. Substitute whatever decorative beads you like, but be sure to match the size to the size listed in the project instructions. I like to use pre-strung bead strands from my local craft store.

Cylinder beads are short, tube-shaped beads with a large open hole and a thin wall. These Japanese beads are uniform in shape and size, and are available in most bead stores. Like seed beads, cylinder beads come in a variety of sizes and colors.

Findings

No jewelry piece is complete without the final touch of the perfect finding! Findings are used to connect, bridge, or embellish jewelry pieces. Sterling silver, copper, gunmetal, brass, and pewter are just some of the metal choices, and the decorative styles are endless. When choosing a finding, keep in mind how it will look with your design and where it will be worn. Also, double-check for any abrasion or tarnishing to the metal before purchasing.

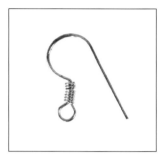

A variety of **clasps** are available for you to use. Before buying a clasp, decide whether the closure will enhance the aesthetic value of the design or the functionality of where it will be worn. A fancier piece of jewelry may call for an extravagant clasp design; an everyday piece of jewelry may need a more secure clasp.

A **jump ring** is a single coil of wire used for connecting other findings or beaded items together. Jump rings come in a variety of gauges and sizes. The sizes may change per project, but I recommend 18-gauge for making jump rings.

Use **earring hooks** to finish a pair of earrings. It's a good idea to get backings too, for added security. You may also choose posts or other styles of earring findings if desired.

Jewelry chain is a delicate chain used for making fringe or necklace rope; you can also extend a piece with chain. Jewelry chain is easy to find in most bead and craft stores and usually comes in a variety of metals. When you purchase jewelry chain, check to see if it is tarnished or damaged. A quality chain has precise loops and no abrasion on the metal.

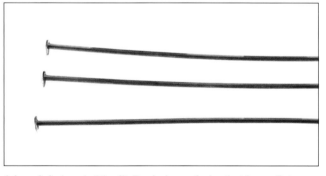

End caps are used to cap off knitted wire. The attached loop allows for attaching a clasp, beads, or components. End caps come in single, double, and even triple strand sizes for all kinds of design possibilities. The special grooves inside the end cap allow the knitted wire to nest securely when crimped. This product was specifically made for just the knitted wire.

A **headpin** is a 1–3 in. (2–7cm) piece of wire that has a flat, round head at one end, similar to a straight pin, but without the sharp point. Headpins are great for making bead baubles (I recommend using 22-gauge headpins). Sometimes a bead hole is too big for a headpin, in which case you'll want to use a bead or crystal to catch the bead and prevent it from sliding off.

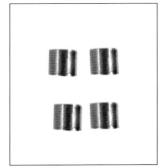

Terminators are used for capping off the ends of capture knitted wire. They may be used for fringe, such as a lariat-style necklace. A terminator has a 3mm diameter opening and special grooves to help hold the capture knitted wire securely when crimped.

A **clamshell** is a type of crimp cover that has two attached-cups with a pin-sized hole between them and there is a hook attached to one of the cups. The idea for this special crimp component is to feed thread or beading wire through the hole and crimp or knot it between the cups. Then the cups are pressed together to conceal everything, and the clasp can be attached to the hook.

A **crimp tube** is a short soft metal cylinder used to secure beading wire. Crimp tubes come in various sizes and metals to choose from. The projects in this book use 2x2mm crimps to keep shopping simple.

Flat crimp ends are used specifically to finish the ends of flat knitted wire. The flat crimp end is 5mm and has an attached loop for connecting a clasp, beads, or components.

Thread and Wire

Different designs call for different construction materials. Some of my designs use beading wire, some use half-hard wire for creating components, and some are stitched with needle and thread. Whatever the design may be, they all have one thing in common, and that's using knitted wire. Listed below are different threads and wires used to make the projects in this book.

Beading wire is a stainless steel cable wire coated with clear nylon plastic. The nylon coating protects the wire from tarnishing, breaking, and makes it comfortable to use. The wire size and flexibility is directly related to the number of cable wires that are twisted together. To make selection easy, I've stuck to the medium sized (0.019 diameter) wire for many of the projects. Beading wire also comes in a variety of colors for you to choose from (the colors were carefully selected to match the color of popular gemstones!).

Half-hard wire usually has a special plating of color over a copper wire core, which is cost-effective and also adds stiffness to the wire.

Use FireLine 6-lb. test as **beading thread** in these jewelry projects. The strength and stiffness of the thread makes it easy to work with and it can go through the tiniest of beads.

TECHNIQUES

This technique guide will explain how to complete the various techniques used to secure, attach, and finish your jewelry designs. Each technique is broken down into a few simplified steps, which is perfect for a beginning beader! So, study up on each technique and be sure to practice until you are comfortable with them.

Attaching New Thread

Sometimes you'll run out of thread mid-project and new thread is necessary to continue stitching. There are a number of ways to attach new thread, but I recommend this particular technique to ensure clean ends when stitching with knitted wire. To add more thread and continue stitching:

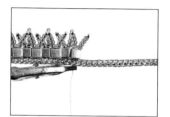

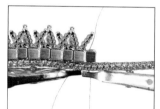

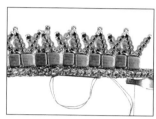

1. Stop stitching when the working thread is about 4 in. (10 cm) long. Release the needle from that thread and place a bead stopper on the old thread, so the stitching doesn't get loose.

2. Re-thread the needle with new thread and place a bead stopper 4 in. (10cm) from the end. Sew through the knitted wire with the new thread at the base of the beadwork, close to the old thread.

3. Continue stitching 5–7 beads, then place a bead stopper at the base of the beadwork on the new thread.

4. Stop stitching and place a bead stopper at the base of the beadwork on the new thread.

Note: A single bead stopper may be used to hold both threads. It just depends on what's comfortable for you.

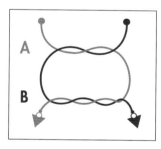

5. Remove the first two bead stoppers and tie a surgeon's knot with those threads.

6. Sew each thread separately into 3 in. (4–6cm) of the knitted wire and trim the extra thread. Remove the second bead stopper and continue stitching.

Note: To tie a surgeon's knot, tie one overhand knot by looping the thread over itself, passing the other thread inside of the loop, and pulling tight to make a knot. Tie another one, except make two twists and pull the threads tight to complete the knot.

Securing Thread

A well-constructed jewelry piece hides all the thread. Before finishing the last stitch of your beaded component, make sure to have at least 6–8 in. (15–20cm) of thread to tie an end knot.

For Separate Ends:

It can be tedious to stitch back through all the beadwork once a project is completed. This technique makes it easy to secure the thread at separate ends, rather than trying to meet them together. To make a knot at separate ends:

1. Finish the last stitch and sew through the knitted wire. Sew up through the next knit-hole, leaving a 2-in. (5cm) loop.

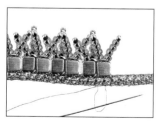

2. Sew through the loop and the knit-hole again, and tighten the thread to get the knot close to the knitted wire.

3. Repeat steps 1 and 2 again, sew the extra thread 3 in. (4–6cm) into the beadwork, and trim.

For Stitched Components:

Sometimes, it's easier to stitch through smaller components of beadwork and meet the end thread with the working thread to tie a knot. To secure the thread for a stitched component:

1. Sew through the knitted wire to meet up with the tail thread.

2. Tie a surgeon's knot with the two threads, sew the extra threads 3 in. (7.6cm) into the beadwork, and trim.

Making Folded Crimps

This technique for crimping is great when stringing large beads with beading wire. To make a folded crimp:

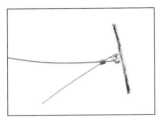 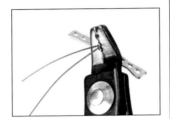

1. String a crimp tube and one half of the clasp on the beading wire. Go back through the crimp, leaving only 1 in. (2.5cm) of extra beading wire.

2. Gently pull the beading wire and use your thumbnail to push the crimp closer to the clasp. Make the beading wire loop about 3mm. This should allow minimal movement of the clasp.

3. Place the crimp inside the second notch of the crimping pliers and gently squeeze. Each wire should sit in one channel of the half-folded crimp.

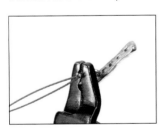 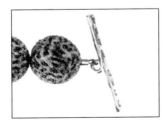

4. Turn the crimp on its side and place it in the first notch of the crimping pliers. Squeeze firmly and remove the pliers. The crimp should look like a cylinder with a seam.

5. String a few beads over the extra beading wire to hide it. To finish the other end, repeat steps 1–6 and go through 1 in. (2.5cm) of the strung beads before tightening the loop. Crimp the tube, and then trim any extra beading wire with the cutters.

Making Flattened Crimps

A flat crimp is useful when needing to hold a single bead or component in place on beading wire. To make a flattened crimp:

 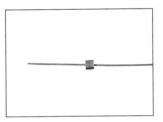

1. String a crimp tube on the beading wire. Gently squeeze the crimp, using chainnose pliers.

2. Release the pliers and examine the crimp to see if it is flattened evenly, like a flat square.

Attaching Clamshells

Clamshells are a great way for hiding a crimp and attaching a finding for lightweight jewelry. To attach a clamshell:

1. Open the clamshell a little bit wider than it is already (this will make it easy to work inside of it).

2. With beading wire, go through the hole between the cups. Pick up a crimp tube and allow the crimp to fall between the cups.

3. Using chainnose pliers, squeeze the crimp so it is flat and trim the extra wire above it.

4. Press the cups together and then attach a clasp onto the hook. Gently fold it in to make it secure.

Attaching End Caps

Knitted wire is different from any other type of wire, cord, or thread and requires a special end cap to finish the ends. This end cap works best for the capture knitted wire or the leather knitted wire. To attach end caps:

1. Trim the knitted wire to a desired length and place the end of the knitted wire into the mouth of the end cap.

2. Use the nylon jaw pliers to gently squeeze the end cap and tug on it to make sure it's secure.

Attaching Flat Crimp Ends

A flat crimp end is perfect for securing the flat knitted wire. The size of this type of crimp is specifically tailored to the width of the flat knitted wire, making it easy to use! To attach a flat crimp end:

1. Insert the flat knitted wire into the mouth of the flat crimp end.

2. Use chainnose pliers to gently press the prongs together and tug on the flat knitted wire to make sure it's secure.

Attaching Terminators

Terminators are great for ending the knitted wire where attaching a component is unnecessary. To attach a terminator:

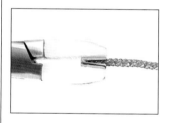 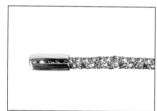

1. Trim the knitted wire to a desired length and place it into the mouth of the terminator.

2. Use nylon jaw pliers to gently squeeze the terminator and tug on it to make sure it is secure.

Making Simple Loops

Simple loops may be used to make fringe, bead baubles, or bridge components together. To make a simple loop for a bead bauble:

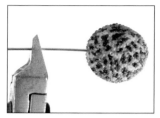

1. Measure ½ in. (1.3cm) of half-hard wire from where the bead stops, and trim the end with cutters.

TIP
If there is too much wire between the bead and wire loop, cut as much wire off from the loop as there is space between the bead and where the loop starts and fold the loop again.

2. Use roundnose pliers to grip the wire at the very tip and rotate them counter-clockwise (away from you) to wrap a coil around the pliers' jaws. If you need to, reposition the pliers to complete a full coil. Release it from the pliers: You have formed a "P" shape.

3. Use chainnose pliers to grip the bottom part of the loop, where the loop begins, and rotate clockwise (toward you) until the loop is centered. In other words, break the neck of the loop so the head is straight. The loop will have a round head with a sharp bend in the neck.

TIP
To open a simple loop, use chainnose pliers to grasp the open part of the loop and gently lift it up towards you. Place your component in the loop and close the loop by pressing the wire back down. If you bend the wire of the loop out, instead of toward you, the loop will lose its shape.

Making Jump Rings

In some instances, you may need to use an odd-sized jump ring, or you can save some costs by making your own! To make jump rings:

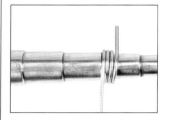

1. Cut 12 in (30cm) of half-hard wire.

2. Coil it tightly around a hand-held mandrel (the size of the jump ring is determined by where it's coiled on the mandrel).

3. Remove the coiled wire from the mandrel and cut straight through the coil with your cutters.

Attaching Jump Rings

Jump rings are useful for bridging components together, especially earrings or bead baubles. To attach a jump ring:

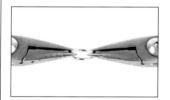

1. Use two chainnose pliers to grasp each side of the jump ring with the seam of the jump ring at the top.

2. Gently push one of the pliers away from you and the other toward you. The open jump ring is now ready to use.

3. Close the jump ring by reversing steps 1 and 2. The jump ring seam should not have any space between it.

Making Wire Scrolls

Add a bit of design while creatively capping off the half-hard wire ends. To make a wire scroll:

1. Measure 3 in. (7.6cm) of half-hard wire from where the bead stops and trim the end with cutters. Run the wire through the nylon jaw pliers to remove any kinks.

2. Use roundnose pliers to grip the wire at the very tip and rotate them counter clockwise, away from you, to wrap a coil around the pliers' jaws. The curl should be at a half "P" shape. Continue folding the wire until it begins to scroll into itself, like a snail shell.

3. Remove the mini-scroll from the roundnose pliers and grasp it firmly with nylon jaw pliers. The wire should point to your left and the mini-scroll should be pointed upwards and partially exposed from the pliers.

4. Pull the wire up onto the scroll. Release the scroll from the pliers and reposition it again to continue making the scroll until all the wire is used.

Hardening Half-Hard Wire

Using the wire jig with half-hard wire is only the first part to making shaped-wire. The second step is to strengthen it to keep it from bending out of place when worn. To harden half-hard wire:

1. Place the wire component on the anvil.

2. Tap the hammer over the wire component a few times. This causes the wire molecules to compress, therefore hardening the wire.

Projects

Urban Beauty
Necklace

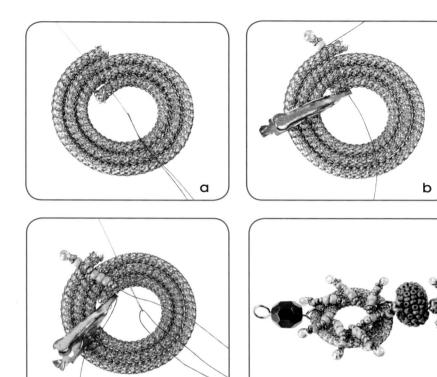

a

b

c

d

Necklace

1. Cut a 11¾-in. (30cm) piece of knitted wire, and make a flat coil that measures approximately ¾ in. (2cm) inside diameter and 1½ in. (4cm) outside diameter.

2. Cut a 24-in. (61cm) piece of beading thread. Thread a beading needle and place a bead stopper 4 in. (10cm) from the end. From the inside of the coil, sew up through where the knitted wire crosses itself **(a)**.

3. Pick up a chartreuse 8º, a 15º, a drop, and a 15º, and sew back through the 8º **(b)**. You have completed one picot stitch.

4. Pick up two 11ºs, three chartreuse 8ºs, and two 11ºs, and sew up through the coil from the inside, so the thread exits the top, approximately ¼ in. (1cm) away from the previous picot **(c)**.

5. Repeat the picot stitch around the coil and secure the thread to finish the coil. Make a total of five coils in 8ºs using alternating colors.

6. Make a total of six smaller coils: Cutting a 5½-in. (14cm) piece of knitted wire. Make a flat coil that measures 1 in. (2.5cm) outside diameter and ½ in. (1.25cm) inside diameter. Repeat the picot stitch, but pick up two 8ºs for the center set of beads. Alternate the 8º colors for each coil.

7. Cut 1¾ in. (4cm) of half-hard wire and make a simple loop on one end. String a decorative bead and make a simple loop on the other end. Repeat for all of the decorative beads. Attach the decorative bead links between the knitted wire coils, alternating between the small and large coils **(d)**. Attach jump rings and the clasp to the end coils to complete the necklace.

TIP
Pass a straight pin or two through the SilverSilk coils to hold the shape in place.

Materials
Necklace: 22 in. (56cm)
- **10** 10–12mm decorative beads
- 4g 2.8mm drop beads, violet gold luster
- 3g 8º seed beads in each of **3** colors: opaque turquoise blue picasso, opaque chartreuse picasso, and opaque brown blue picasso
- 3g 11º seed beads, matte metallic dark gold
- 3g 15º seed beads, matte metallic dark bronze
- toggle clasp
- **2** 10mm jump rings
- 2 ft. (61cm) 20-gauge half-hard wire
- 8 ft. (2.4m) capture knitted wire, pearlesque AB hematite

Techniques
- Securing thread for stitched components (p. 14)
- Making simple loops (p. 16)
- Making and attaching jump rings (p. 16)

Orange Spice
Earrings

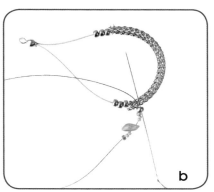

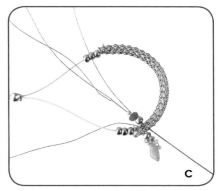

Earrings

1. Cut a 6-in. (15cm) piece of beading wire and a 2-in. (5cm) piece of knitted wire. With the beading wire, pick up three 8°s, the knitted wire, and three 8°s. Gather both ends and string a clamshell. String a crimp bead and make a folded crimp **(a)**. Close the clamshell over the crimp.

2. Cut 24 in. (61cm) of beading thread. Thread a beading needle and place a bead stopper 4 in. (10cm) from the end. Starting from the left end, sew down through the knitted wire and pick up an 8°, an 11°, two 15°s, a long magatama, two 15°s, and an 11°. Sew up through the 8° and the knitted wire **(b)**. You have completed one picot stitch.

3. Pick up an 8°, a crystal, and a 15°. Sew back through the crystal, 8° and the knitted wire, but angle the needle so the thread exits next to the last picot stitch **(c)**.

4. Repeat the top and bottom picot stitch to the end of the knitted wire and secure the thread.

5. Make a second earring. Attach the earring hooks to the loops of the clamshells to finish.

Materials
Earrings: 2½ in. (6cm)
- **22** 4x7mm long magatamas, matte transparent orange AB
- **18** 4mm faceted round crystals, opaque fuchsia
- 2g 8° seed beads, bright copper
- 2g 11° seed beads, silver-lined orange AB
- 2g 15° seed beads, matte sea green
- pair of earring hooks
- **2** clamshells
- **2** 2mm crimp tubes
- 12 in. (30cm) beading wire, .019, fluorite
- 4 in. (10cm) hollow knitted wire, bronze

Techniques
- Securing thread for stitched components (p. 14)
- Making a folded crimp (p. 14)
- Attaching a clamshell (p. 15)

Midnight
Rendezvous
Necklace

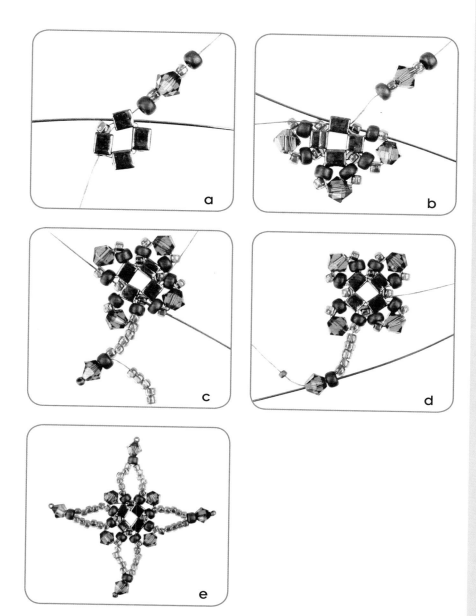

Materials

Necklace: 22 in. (56cm)

- **6** 6–15mm decorative beads
- **3** 10mm faceted barrel crystals, golden crystal shadow AB
- **3** 6mm faceted roundel crystals, sand
- **12** 4mm bicone crystals, montana blue
- **12** 3mm cube beads, metallic bronze
- **2g** 8º seed beads, matte metallic dark-raspberry iris
- **2g** 15º seed beads, emerald-lined cobalt AB
- **1g** 15º seed beads, matte metallic dark-bronze
- toggle clasp
- **2** flat crimp ends
- **7** 4mm jump rings
- 20 in. (51cm) jewelry chain, 1mm links
- 24 in. (61cm) 20-gauge half-hard wire
- 1 yd. (.9m) flat knitted wire, vintage bronze
- 24 in. (61cm) flat knitted wire, bronze

Techniques
- Securing thread for stitched components (p. 14)
- Attaching flat crimp ends (p. 15)
- Making simple loops (p. 16)
- Making and attaching jump rings (p. 16)

Beaded Stars

1. Cut a 24-in. (61cm) piece of beading thread. Thread a beading needle and place a bead stopper 4 in. (10cm) from the end. Pick up four cubes and sew through the first cube to make a loop. Pick up an 11º and sew through the next cube. Pick up an 8º, an 11º, a bicone, an 11º, and an 8º, and sew through the cube bead again to make a loop **(a)**. Repeat the stitch for the other three cubes, making sure to sew one 11º between each cube.

2. Complete the last loop and then sew through the first 8º and 11º of the first loop **(b)**. Pick up five 11ºs, an 8º, a bicone, and a 15º. Sew back though the bicone and 8º, and pick up five 11sº **(c)**. Sew through the 11º and 8º of the last loop, then through the 11º (between the cube beads), the cube bead, and the next 11º. Sew through the 8º and 11º of the third loop **(d)**.

3. Pick up five 11ºs and repeat the stitch to complete the other corners. Secure the thread **(e)**. Make two more beaded stars and set them aside.

TIP
Make a chain tassel by cutting the jewelry chain into 10 2-in. (5cm) pieces, and then attaching them to a jump ring. Feel free to attach a small decorative bead or two to the chain tassel for fun!

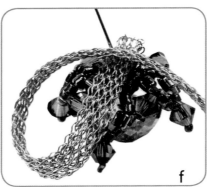

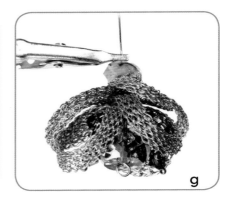

Beaded Flowers

4. Cut a 12-in. (30cm) piece of bronze flat knitted wire and a 3-in. (7.6cm) piece of half-hard wire. Make a simple loop on one end of the half-hardwire. Then pick up a barrel bead, a beaded star, and the end of the flat knitted wire. Make a loop with the flat knitted wire by going through a knit-hole about 2 in. (5cm) from the end **(f)**. Use the rest of the flat knitted wire to make five or six loops, graduating in size from large loops to small.

5. String a 6mm rondelle and make a simple loop to finish the beaded flower **(g)**. Make two more beaded flowers.

Finishing

6. Attach the flat crimp ends and clasp to the vintage bronze flat knitted wire. Attach the beaded flowers, decorative beads, and chain tassel together using jump rings to complete the necklace.

Seduction
in Bronze
Bracelet

Materials
Bracelet: 7 in. (18cm)
- **4** 10–12mm decorative beads
- 3g 8mm flower sequins, matte bronze
- **24** 6mm faceted rondelle crystals, metallic bronze
- 4g 3.8mm heishi beads, metallic bronze
- 3g 11º seed beads, bright copper
- 2g 15º seed beads, matte silver-lined gold
- **2** 12mm bead caps
- toggle clasp
- **2** 2mm crimp tubes
- 4mm jump ring
- 1 ft. (30cm) beading wire, .014, antique bronze
- 5½ in. (14cm) 7mm hollow knitted wire, Andromeda

Techniques
- Securing thread for separate ends (p. 13)
- Making folded crimps (p. 14)
- Making and attaching jump rings (p. 16)

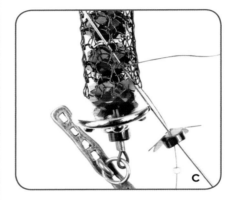

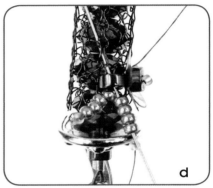

Bracelet

1. Crimp one half of the clasp to one end of the beading wire and string four decorative beads, a bead cap, and 24 6mm crystals. Pass the knitted wire over the crystals, and string a bead cap and a heishi bead. Crimp the other clasp half to the other end of the beading wire **(a)**.

Note: Make sure to adjust the tension of the bracelet to curve around your wrist before crimping or it will not fit correctly.

2. Cut a 24-in. (61cm) piece of beading thread. Thread a beading needle and place a bead stopper 4 in. (10cm) from the end. At the end of the knitted wire, sew through a knit-hole **(b)**. Pick up a sequin, a heishi, and a 15º, and sew back through the heishi and sequin. Sew through the knit-hole that is one left and three above from where the first picot stitch was made **(c)**. You have completed one picot stitch.

3. Pick up a heishi, four 11ºs, and a 15º, and sew back through the four 11ºs. Pick up four 11ºs and a 15º, and sew back through the 11º and the heishi **(d)**. Sew through the next diagonal knit-hole (see step 2), and alternate between the picot stitches to the end of the knitted wire. Secure the thread to complete the bracelet.

TIP
The open knit-holes are great for sewing anywhere! Feel free to make up your own stitching pattern.

Evergreen

Bracelet

Materials

Bracelet: 7½ in. (19cm)

- **2** 12mm decorative beads
- **24** 4x7mm long magatama, matte green AB
- 3g 8° seed beads in each of **2** colors: bright copper and opaque chartreuse picasso
- 4g 11° seed beads, silver-lined emerald AB
- 3g 11°, opaque turquoise
- **2** double-strand end caps
- toggle clasp
- 4 in. (10cm) 20-gauge half-hard wire
- 11 in. (28cm) leather knitted wire

Techniques

- Securing thread for stitched components (p. 14)
- Attaching end caps (p. 15)
- Making simple loops (p. 16)

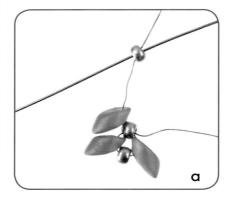

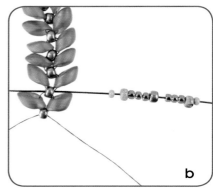

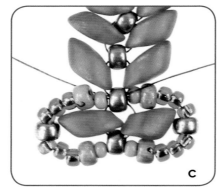

Bracelet

1. Cut a 3-ft. (1m) piece of beading thread. Thread a needle at both ends. Pick up a bright copper 8° seed bead and position it in the center of the thread. Pick up one long magatama on each needle and with one needle, pick up a copper 8°. Cross the other needle through it to make a loop in the middle of the thread.

2. Pick up a long magatama on each needle and then pick up a copper 8° on one of the needles. Cross the other needle through it to make the second loop **(a)**. Repeat this stitch until you have added all of the long magatamas.

3. On both needles, pick up an opaque turquoise 11°, a chartreuse 8°, three emerald 11°s, a copper 8°, three emerald 11°s, a chartreuse 8°, and a turquoise 11°. Sew through the next-to-last stitched copper 8° **(b, c)**.

Note: Be sure to adjust the long magatamas to face forward as the stitches are made.

4. Repeat the stitch to the last copper 8° and secure the thread.

5. Cut two 5½-in. (14cm) pieces of knitted wire and gently pass each of them through the bead loops **(d)**. Meet the ends together and attach the end caps.

6. Cut 2 in. (5cm) of half-hard wire and make a simple loop on one end. String a 12mm decorative bead and make another simple loop. Repeat to make a second beaded link. Attach a beaded link to an end cap and a clasp half at each end of the bracelet.

TIP

I pre-strung each of the 28 long magatamas so that they faced the same direction before I stitched them in place. It saved me so much time trying to figure out if they faced the same direction while stitching.

Into the Wild
Necklace

a

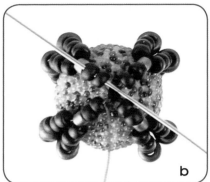

b

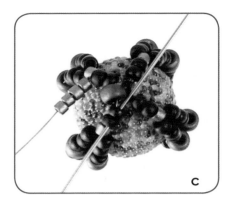

c

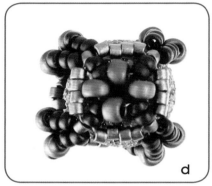

d

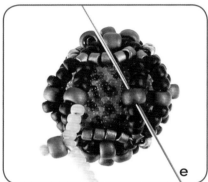

e

f

g

Five Beaded Beads

1. Cut a 24-in. piece (61cm) of beading thread. Thread a beading needle and place a bead stopper 4 in. (10cm) from the end. Pick up a round bead, two 11°s, a cylinder, three 11°s, an 8°, three 11°s, a cylinder, and two 11°s. Sew up through the round bead and then through the top two 11°s and cylinder. Pick up three 11°s, an 8°, and three 11°s, sew through the last cylinder and two 11°s **(a)**, and sew up through the round bead again. You have completed one bead loop.

2. Repeat the bead loops three more times for a total of four bead loops around the round bead. With the thread exiting two 11°s, pick up an 8° and sew up through two 11°s to the left **(b)**.

3. Pick up four cylinders and sew up through the two 11°s **(c)**. Sew through the 8° and two 11°s again and pick up four cylinders. Repeat to add four sets of 8°s in the center with cylinders below them **(d)**.

4. Sew through an 8° in the middle of the round bead, pick up five 15°s, an 8°, and a 15°, and sew back through the 8°. Pick up five 15°s and sew up through the next middle 8° **(e)**. Repeat this stitch and then sew through the first 8° again to complete the round of fringe. Sew through the 11°s to reach another 8° and make another round of fringe. Complete the fringe on all four sets of bead loops and secure the thread to finish the beaded bead **(f, g)**. Make four more beaded beads.

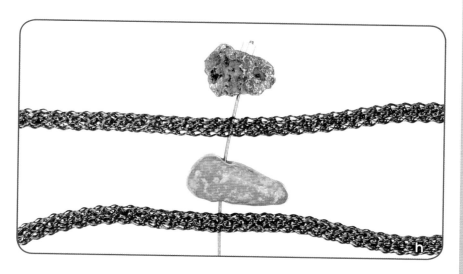

Finishing

5. Cut a 22-in. (56cm) piece of knitted wire. Attach the clasp and end caps to the knitted wire, with the shorter knitted wire as the inner strand.

6. Cut a 6-in. (15cm) piece of beading wire and make a flattened crimp at the tip. String a pyrite bead and go through the inner knitted wire at the center of the necklace. String a mud bead and go through the outer knitted wire **(h)**. Place a bead stopper to hold the beading wire in place. Repeat this step to make a total of twelve strands, each tapering as they move away from the center.

7. Arrange the decorative beads and beaded beads on the twelve strands, then secure them in place with flattened crimps to complete the necklace.

Materials

Necklace: 22 in. (56cm)

- **5** 12mm round beads
- **16** 10mm cone-shaped mud beads
- **14** 8–12mm decorative beads
- **20** 6–10mm pyrite beads
- 3g 8º seed beads, matte opaque olivine
- 4g 11º seed beads in each of **2** colors: matte black and matte metallic bronze
- 3g 15º seed beads, matte opaque dark cream
- **2** double-strand end caps
- **30** 2mm crimp tubes
- **2** 4mm jump rings
- toggle clasp
- 4 ft. (1.2m) beading wire, .019, vintage bronze
- 4 ft. capture knitted wire, vintage bronze

Techniques

- Securing thread for stitched components (p. 14)
- Making flattened crimps (p. 14)
- Attaching end caps (p. 15)
- Making and attaching jump rings (p. 16)

Tangerine
Torrent
Bracelet

a

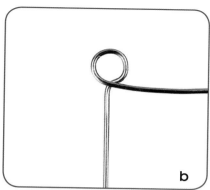
b

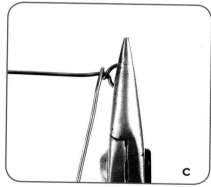
c

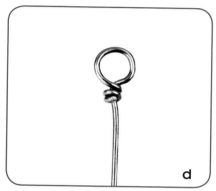
d

Bracelet

1. Cut a 24-in. (61cm) piece of beading thread. Thread a beading needle and place a bead stopper 4 in. (10cm) from the end. Start ½ in. (1cm) from the end of the hollow knitted wire and sew through a knit-hole.

2. Pick up an 8º seed bead, a 15º seed bead, a drop bead, and a 15º, and sew back through the 8º and through the next knit-hole up **(a)**. You have completed one picot stitch. Repeat the picot stitch to the end of the knitted wire. Secure the thread and make three more beaded knitted wires.

3. Cut a 12-in. (30cm) piece of half-hard wire and began to make a simple loop 2 in. (5cm) from the end, but don't trim the extra wire; instead, it should overlap the base wire **(b)**.

4. Hold the eye with chainnose pliers and coil the wire around the base wire twice. Trim the extra wire **(c, d)**.

Materials
Bracelet: 8 in. (20cm)
- **8** 10–20mm decorative beads
- **8** 6mm faceted rondelle crystals, burnt orange AB
- 4g 3.4mm drop beads, matte transparent orange AB
- 4g 8º seed beads, matte hot pink
- 3g 15º seed beads, matte transparent lavender
- toggle clasp
- 4mm jump ring
- 2 yd. (1.8m) 20-gauge half-hard wire
- 32 in. (81cm) hollow knitted wire, hematite

Techniques
- Securing thread for separate ends (p. 13)
- Making simple loops (p. 16)
- Making and attaching jump rings (p. 16)

5. On the wire, string a faceted bead, a decorative bead, and a faceted bead, and make another wire-wrapped loop at the end (again, don't trim the extra wire after making the coil) **(e)**.

6. String the beaded knitted wire over the wire and gently twist it around the decorative bead twice **(f)**. Coil the wire over the first wire-wrapped loop twice and trim **(g)**.

7. Cut a 1¾-in. (4cm) piece of half-hard wire and make a simple loop on one end. String a decorative bead and make another simple loop. Attach the decorative beads between each wire-wrapped bead. Attach a clasp clasp on each end (use a 4mm jump ring, if necessary) to complete the bracelet.

Ampersand
Earrings

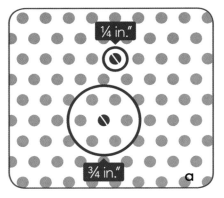

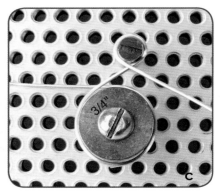

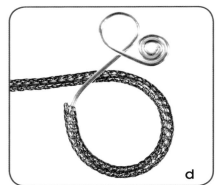

Earrings

1. Attach the ¼-in. (6mm) and ¾-in. (1.9mm) pegs on the jig as shown **(a)**.

2. Cut a 12-in. (30cm) piece of half-hard wire and measure 4 in. (10cm) from the end. Make a single coil around the ¾-in. peg. The longer part of wire should be below the ¼-in. peg **(b, c)**.

3. Coil the longer wire around the ¼-in. peg and remove it from the jig. Make a wire scroll with the rest of that wire.

4. Cut a 3-in. (7.6cm) piece of knitted wire and string it over the wire **(d)**. Make a wire scroll with the rest of that wire, gently coiling and sculpting it to the center of the larger loop **(e)**.

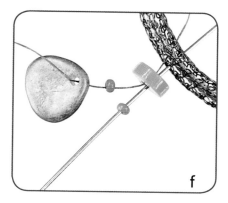 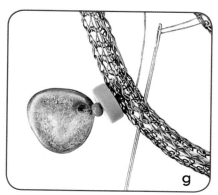

5. Cut a 24-in. (61cm) piece of beading thread. Thread a beading needle and place a bead stopper 4 in. (10cm) from the end. Starting just below the smaller loop, sew down through the knitted wire and pick up a heishi, a 15º seed bead, a petal, and a 15º, and sew back through the heishi and knitted wire **(f)**. You have completed one picot stitch.

6. Sew back through the knitted wire without any beads, but angle the needle so the thread exits next to the last picot stitch **(g)**.

7. Continue making picot stitches to the end of the knitted wire. Secure the thread. Attach an earring hook to complete the earring.

8. Make a second earring.

Materials

Earrings: 2½ in. (6cm)

- **24** 5mm petal beads, forest green luster
- **24** 4mm heishi beads, turquoise
- 1g 15º seed beads, opaque coral
- pair of earring hooks
- 24 in. (61cm) 18-gauge half-hard wire
- 6 in. (81cm) hollow knitted wire, olivine
- Now that's a Jig!*
  ¼ in. (5mm) peg
  ¾ in. (1cm) peg

You can substitute a WigJig or another peg-based tool for this project.

Techniques

- Securing thread for stitched components (p. 14)
- Making simple loops (p. 16)
- Making wire scrolls (p. 17)
- Hardening half-hard wire (p. 17)

Scorpio
Necklace

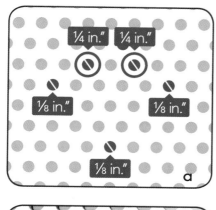

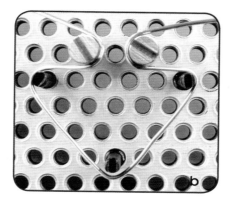

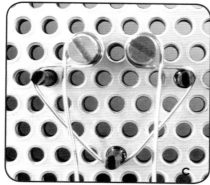

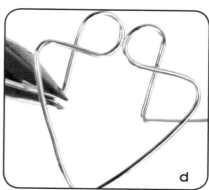

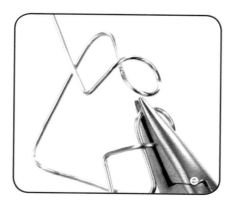

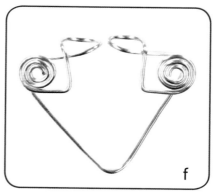

Materials

Necklace: 24 in. (61cm)

- **6** 10–15mm decorative beads
- **2** 6mm crystal drops
- 4g 3.5mm long drop beads, matte yellow gold
- 2g 11º seed beads, silver-lined gold AB
- 2g 15º seed beads, dyed opaque pumpkin
- toggle clasp
- **4** single-strand end caps
- **3** 2-in. (5cm) headpins
- **2** 5mm jump rings
- 36 in. (91cm) 18-gauge half-hard wire
- 4 in. (10cm) 24-gauge half-hard wire
- 36 in. (91cm) capture knitted wire, olivine
- Now that's a Jig!*
  2 ¼-in. (5mm) pegs
  3 ⅛-in. (3.2mm) pegs

You can substitute a WigJig or another peg-based tool for this project.

Techniques

- Securing thread for stitched components (p. 14)
- Attaching end caps (p. 15)
- Making and attaching jump rings (p. 16)
- Making wire scrolls (p. 17)
- Hardening half-hard wire (p. 17)

Necklace

1. Attach the ¼-in. and ⅛-in. pegs on the jig as shown **(a)**.

2. Cut an 18-in. (46cm) piece of 18-gauge wire and center the wire under the bottom middle peg. Wrap the wire around the outside of the three outer ⅛-in. pegs, and then around the inside of the ¼-in. pegs as shown **(b)**.

3. Wrap the wire tails around the ¼-in. pegs and down toward the starting point **(c)**. Remove the wire component from the jig and work-harden it. Use chainnose pliers to bend the wire ends out at a 90-degree angle about ½ in. (1cm) below the loops **(d)**.

4. Hold the loop (or "eye") with chainnose pliers and bend the eye back at a 45-degree angle. Repeat for the other loop **(e)**. Make a scroll with each remaining wire end **(f)**.

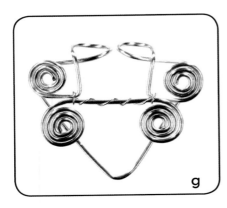

g

h

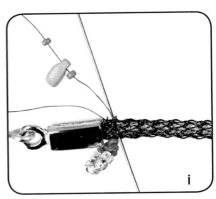

i

j

5. Cut an 8-in. (20cm) piece of 22-gauge wire and make a scroll at each end, leaving a 1-in. (2.5cm) gap between them. Connect the bar to the main wire component by wrapping 24-gauge half-hard wire around the base of the wire scrolls and the gap between the scrolls from step 4 **(g)**.

6. Cut 1¾-in. (4.4cm) piece of 18-gauge wire and make a simple loop on one end. String a decorative bead and make another simple loop. Repeat to make four decorative bead links. String a crystal drop on a headpin and make a simple loop.

7. Cut a 3-in. (7.6cm) piece of knitted wire and attach an end cap to each end. Cut a 24-in. (61cm) of beading thread. Thread the beading needle and place a bead stopper 4 in. (10cm) from the end. Sew through the knitted wire close to the end cap and pick up three 15º seed beads, five 11º seed beads, and three 15ºs. Sew back down through the knitted wire **(h)**. You have completed one picot stitch.

8. Pick up a 15º, a drop bead, and a 15º, and sew up through the knitted wire to make another picot stitch **(i)**. Continue, alternating the two picot stitches randomly on the knitted wire in all directions. Leave larger spaces between the picot stitches toward one end. Secure the thread.

9. Attach the decorative bead links and knitted wire component as desired (see main photo for placement) to make a long beaded pendant.

10. With the remaining piece of knitted wire, attach an end cap to each end. Attach a clasp half to each end cap (use 5mm jump rings, if necessary). Find the middle and go through the space between the top wire scrolls, then up through the 45-degree wire loops. Pull the knitted wire up to match the ends evenly.

11. Make three additional bead baubles by stringing each remaining decorative bead and crystal drop on a headpin. Cut a 1½-in. (3.8cm) piece of 18-gauge wire and make a simple loop on one end. String a bead bauble, go through the knitted wire (just above where the wire component starts), and make another simple loop. Attach a bead bauble to each simple loop. Attach the long beaded pendant to the knitted wire loop to complete the necklace **(j)**.

Rorschach
Bracelet

a

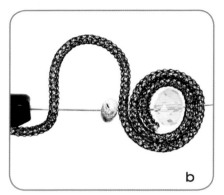

b

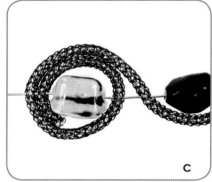

c

d

e

f

Bracelet

1. Cut a 13-in. (33cm) piece of knitted wire and make a 1-in. (2.5cm) coil on one end. Use a straight pin to hold the coil in place **(a)**.

2. Cut a 3½-in. (9cm) piece of half-hard wire and make a simple loop on one end. Pass the other end through the knitted wire, string an 8–10mm decorative bead (so it's nested inside the coil), and then pass through the knitted wire again. String a 6mm decorative bead and measure out 2½ in. (6cm) of knitted wire. Pass the half-hard wire through the knitted wire and snug up the wire to form a loop **(b)**.

3. String an 8–12mm decorative bead and measure out 1¾ in. (4.4cm) of knitted wire. Pass the half-hard wire through the knitted wire to form a second loop **(c)**.

4. Make a 1-in. (2.5cm) coil with the rest of the knitted wire, and pass the half-hard wire through it (string an 8–10mm decorative bead so it's nested inside the coil). Push the knitted wire coils and loops together and make a simple loop close to the coil **(d)**.

5. Cut a 36-in. (91cm) piece of beading thread. Thread a beading needle and place a bead stopper 4 in. (10cm) from the end. With the longest loop pointing down, start on the left side below the simple loop and sew down through the knitted wire coils. Pick up a 3mm crystal rondelle, two 11º seed beads, an 8º seed bead, and a 15º, and sew back through the 8º, the two 11ºs, the crystal, and the knitted wire **(e)**. You have completed one picot stitch.

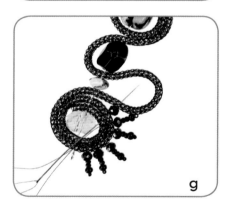

g

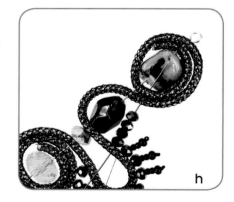

h

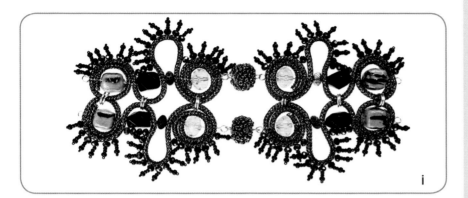

i

6. Sew down through the knitted wire, but angle the needle so the thread exits next to the last picot stitch **(f)**. Continue making picot stitches to the end of the knitted wire. To stitch onto the next loop, pick up a crystal and sew through the knitted wire of the next loop **(g)**. To stitch to the last knitted wire coil, pick up four crystals and sew through the knitted wire of the last coil **(h)**. You have completed one beaded knitted wire link. Make three more links.

7. Cut a 1¾-in. (4.4cm) piece of wire. Make a simple loop on one end, string a 12mm decorative bead, and make another simple loop. Repeat to make six decorative bead links.

8. Attach the beaded knitted wire links, jump rings, decorative beads, and clasp halves together to complete the bracelet **(i)**.

Materials
Bracelet: 8 in. (20cm)
- **6** 12mm decorative beads
- **16** 8–10mm decorative beads
- **125** 3mm rondelle crystals
- 3g 8º seed beads, opaque black
- 3g 11º seed beads, matte charcoal
- 1g 15º seed beads, opaque black
- **2** two-part magnetic clasps
- **12** 6mm jump rings
- 24 in. (61cm) 22-gauge half-hard wire
- 4½ ft. (1.4m) 3mm capture knitted wire, black

Techniques
- Securing thread for separate ends (p. 13)
- Making simple loops (p. 16)
- Making and attaching jump rings (p. 16)

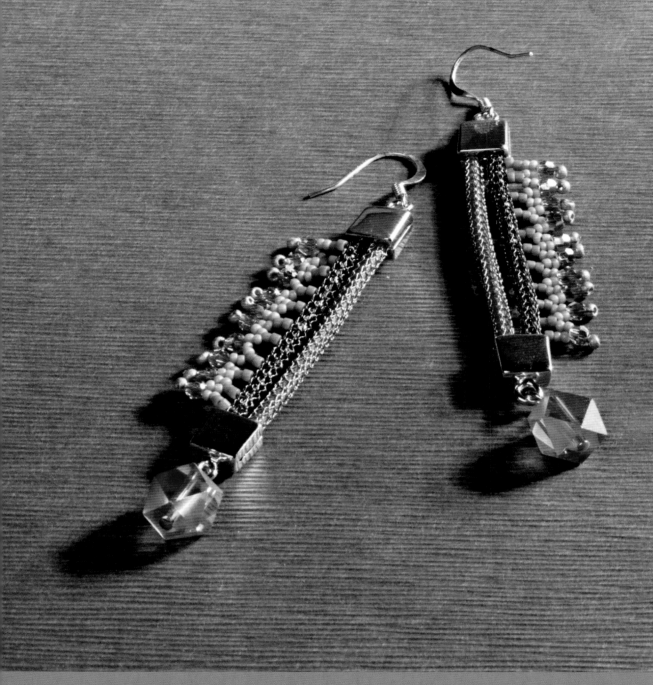

Native
Impressions
Earrings

a

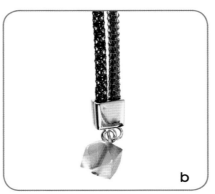

b

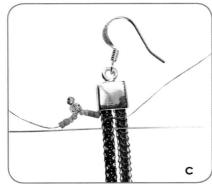

c

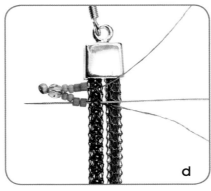

d

Materials

Earrings: 2³/₄ in. (7cm)

- **2** 6mm decorative beads
- **20** 3mm faceted round crystals
- 1g 11º cylinder beads, opaque slate blue
- 1g 11º seed beads, matte yellow gold
- 1g 15º seed beads, matte aqua
- pair of earring hooks
- **4** double-strand end caps
- **2** 1-in. (2.5cm) headpins
- 4 in. (10cm) capture knitted wire, olivine
- 4 in. leather knitted wire, tan/gold

Techniques

- Securing thread for stitched components (p. 14)
- Making simple loops (p. 16)
- Attaching end caps (p. 15)

Earrings

1. Cut a 2-in. (5cm) piece of each knitted wire. Place the knitted wires side by side and attach an end cap on each end. Attach an earring hook to one end cap **(a)**. On a headpin, string a 6mm decorative bead and make a simple loop. Attach the dangle to the other end cap **(b)**.

2. Cut a 24-in. (61cm) piece of beading thread. Thread a beading needle and place a bead stopper 4 in. (10cm) from the end. Sew through the capture knitted wire close to the top end cap, and pick up two cylinders, two 15º seed beads, a crystal, and an 11º seed bead. Sew back through the crystal. Pick up two 15ºs and two cylinders, and sew through the capture knitted wire 2–3mm from the crystal. You have completed one picot stitch **(c)**.

3. Sew down through the capture knitted wire again without picking up any beads (this will anchor the thread around the chain inside the knitted wire). Sew through the last two 11ºs again to start another picot stitch **(d)**.

Note: Make sure you don't sew through the same knit-hole where the thread exited last or the beadwork will come undone.

4. Continue making picot stitches to the end of the capture knitted wire. Secure the thread to finish the earring. Make another earring.

Ferntasia
Bracelet

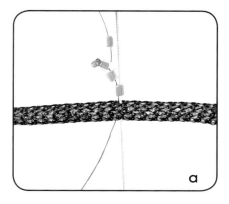

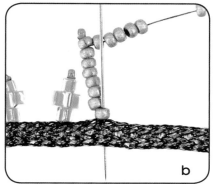

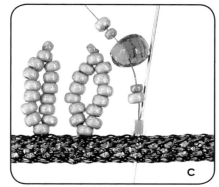

Materials
Bracelet: 7 in. (18cm)

- 2g 4mm magatama beads, mint green-lined sapphire
- 3g 1.8mm cube beads, transparent mint-lined
- 3g 11º seed beads, matte yellow gold
- 2g 15º seed beads, dyed opaque pumpkin
- **2** short terminators
- 27 in. (69cm) capture knitted wire, pearlesque AB emerald

Techniques
- Securing thread for separate ends (p. 13)
- Attaching terminators (p. 15)

Bracelet

1. Attach a short terminator to each end of the knitted wire.

2. Cut a 5-ft. (1.5m) piece of beading thread. Thread a beading needle and place a bead stopper 4 in. (10cm) from the end. Sew through a knit-hole close to a terminator. Pick up three cube beads and a 15º seed bead and sew back through the last cube. Pick up another cube and sew back through the first cube and the knitted wire **(a)**. You have completed one picot stitch. Sew up through the knitted wire ¼ in. (1cm) from the previous picot stitch. Make picot stitches on the knitted wire for 9 in. (23cm).

3. Change the pattern: Pick up nine 11º seed beads and a 15º. Sew back through the last 11º, pick up six 11ºs, and then sew through the first 11º and the knitted wire **(b)**. Make these picot stitches on the knitted wire for 9 in. (23cm).

4. Make the last pattern: Pick up a cube, an 11º, a 15º, a magatama, a 15º, and an 11º. Sew back through the cube and knitted wire **(c)**. Make these picot stitches to the end of the knitted wire and then secure the thread.

5. Make a stacked coil with the beaded knitted wire, matching up the beginning and the ending of each picot stitch variation. Use a straight pin to hold them in place. Cut a 24-in. (60cm) piece of beading thread and thread a needle. Place a bead stopper 4 in. (10cm) from the end and sew through the coils around the bracelet **(d)**. Secure the thread to complete the bracelet.

TIP
Sew straight through just the top knit-holes to help hide the working thread as you stitch the picots.

Sweet
Impression
Necklace

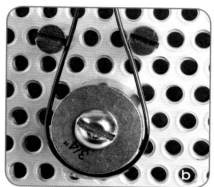

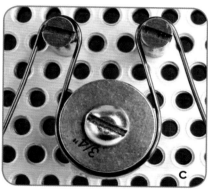

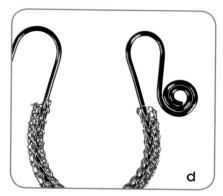

Necklace

1. Attach the ¼-in. and ¾-in. pegs on the jig as shown **(a)**.

2. Cut 8 in. (20cm) of half-hard wire. Center the wire under the bottom middle peg and wrap up toward the top two pegs to make a U shape **(b)**.

3. Wrap the wire ends around the top two pegs from inside to outside **(c)**. Remove the wire component from the jig and make a small wire scroll that points outward on one end. Harden the scroll and U-shape, and then cut a 2½-in. (6.4cm) piece of knitted wire and string it on the component **(d)**. Make another wire scroll on the other end and harden the remaining wire.

Materials
Necklace: 18 in. (46cm)
- **11** 15mm decorative beads
- 5g 3x5.5mm long drop beads, matte transparent peach AB
- **120** 4mm flat faceted beads, pink rose
- 5g 11º seed beads, opaque luster dark mauve
- 8g 11º seed beads, dark rose silver-lined alabaster
- 4g 15º seed beads, gold
- toggle clasp
- **12** 8mm jump rings
- 7½ ft. (2m) 20-gauge half-hard wire
- 36 in. (1m) hollow knitted wire, bronze
- Now that's a Jig!*
  2 ¼ in. (6mm) pegs
  ¾ in. (1cm) peg

You can substitute a WigJig or another peg-based tool for this project.

Techniques
- Securing thread for stitched components (p. 14)
- Making and attaching jump rings (p. 16)
- Making wire scrolls (p. 17)
- Hardening half-hard wire (p. 17)

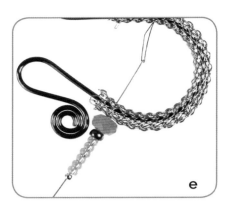

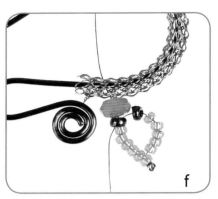

e

f

g

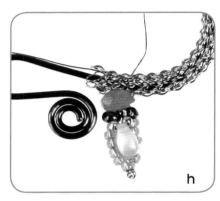

h

4. Cut a 24-in. (61cm) piece of beading thread. Thread a beading needle and place a bead stopper 4 in. (10cm) from the end. Sew through one end of the knitted wire and pick up a faceted bead, a mauve 11º seed bead, six pink 11º seed beads, and a 15º seed bead **(e)**.

5. Sew back through the last pink 11º, pick up five pink 11ºs, and a mauve 11º, and sew down through the first mauve 11º **(f)**.

6. Pick up a 15º, a drop bead, and a 15º, and sew up through the second mauve 11º, the faceted bead, and the knitted wire **(g, h)**. You have completed one picot stitch.

7. Sew back through the knitted wire without any beads, but angle the needle so the thread exits next to the last picot stitch.

8. Repeat the picot stitch to the end of the knitted wire. Stitch the decorative bead in the center: Sew down through ½ in. (1.3cm) of the knitted wire and exit through a knit-hole on the beaded wire component that faces inside. Pick up a decorative bead and sew through the knitted wire on the other side. Secure the thread to finish the component.

9. Make ten more beaded components and use jump rings to attach them together (go through the wire scrolls). Attach a clasp to complete the necklace.

Starburst
Earrings

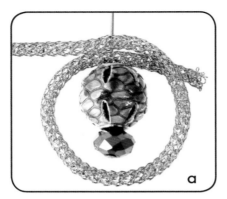

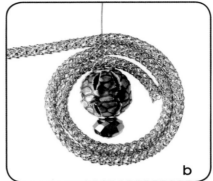

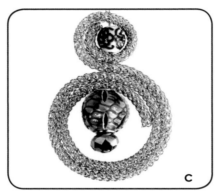

Earrings

1. Cut a 11½-in. (29cm) piece of knitted wire. On a headpin, string a crystal and a 15mm decorative bead and then go through the knitted wire ¾ in. (2cm) from the end. Go through the knitted wire 2¾ in. (7cm) from that point to form a loop **(a)**.

2. Coil the knitted wire close to the first loop and go through it **(b)**.

3. Make a small coil with the remaining knitted wire and pass the headpin through the coil, picking up a 7mm decorative bead (so that it's nested inside the coil) **(c)**. Make a simple loop at the end of the headpin.

4. Cut an 18-in. (46cm) piece of beading thread. Thread a beading needle and place a bead stopper 4 in. (10cm) from the end. Starting on the top right side, sew up through the knitted wire coils and pick up an 8° seed bead and a cobalt 11° seed bead **(d)**. Sew back through the 8° and the knitted wire. You have completed the first picot stitch.

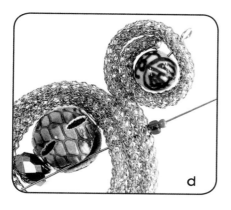

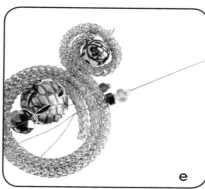

5. Sew up through the knitted wire, pick up a heishi, an aqua 11º seed bead, a magatama bead, and an aqua 11º, and then sew back through the heishi and the knitted wire **(e)**. You have completed the second picot stitch.

6. Alternate picot stitches around the knitted wire coil and secure the thread to finish. Attach an earring hook to the top simple loop. Make a second earring.

Materials
Earrings: 2¼ in. (7.5cm)
- **2** 15mm decorative beads
- **2** 8mm faceted rondelle crystals, bronze
- **2** 7mm decorative beads
- **18** 4mm magatama beads, mint green-lined sapphire
- **18** 4mm heishi beads, metallic bronze
- 1g 8º seed beads, silver-lined cobalt
- 1g 11º seed beads in each of **2** colors: opaque cobalt and mint-lined aqua
- pair of earring wires
- **2** 3-in. (7.6cm) headpins
- 23 in. (58cm) capture knitted wire, chartreuse

Techniques
- Securing thread for stitched components (p. 14)
- Making simple loops (p. 16)

Nouveau
Bracelet

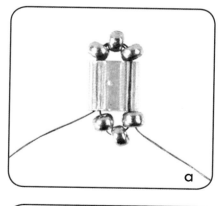

a

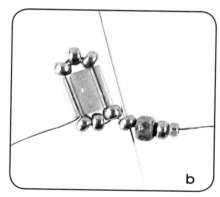

b

c

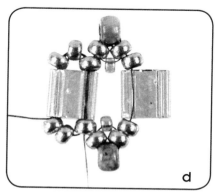

d

Materials
Bracelet: 6½ in. (16.5cm)
- **4** 6–10mm decorative beads
- 3g 3x5.5mm long drop beads, matte metallic khaki iris
- 3g 2.8mm dagger beads, transparent amethyst
- 3g Tila beads, violet luster
- 3g 8º seed beads, opaque turquoise blue picasso
- 4g 11º seed beads, bright copper
- 2g 15º seed beads, transparent violet luster
- three-hole slide clasp
- **4** flat-crimp ends
- **4** 2-in. (5cm) headpins
- **4** 4mm jump rings
- 14 in. (36cm) flat knitted wire, antique copper

Techniques
- Securing thread for separate ends (p. 13)
- Making simple loops (p. 16)
- Attaching flat crimp ends (p. 15)
- Making and attaching jump rings (p. 16)

Bracelet

1. Cut a 6½-ft. (2m) piece of beading thread. Thread a beading needle and place a bead stopper 6 in. (15cm) from the end. Sew up through the left hole of a Tila bead and pick up three 11º seed beads. Sew down through the right hole, pick up three 11ºs, and then sew up through left hole again. Sew through the three 11ºs, and then sew down through the right hole of the Tila and an 11º **(a)**.

2. Pick up an 11º, an 8º seed bead, an 11º, and a 15º, and sew through the first 11º **(b)**.

3. Skip the 8º and sew through the next 11º. You have completed one picot stitch.

4. Pick up an 11º, a Tila, two 11ºs, an 8º, an 11º, and a 15º **(c)**. Sew through the first 11º, skip the 8º, and sew through the next 11º, as in step 3. Then sew through the 11º and the right hole of the first Tila **(d)**.

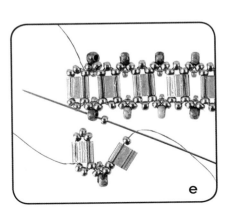

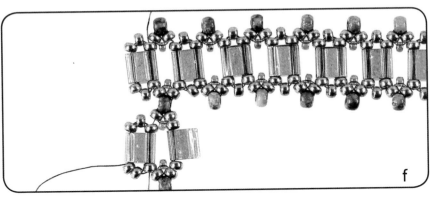

e

f

5. Sew through the beads to reach the top right 11° above the second Tila. Repeat steps 2–4 to sew 23 Tilas together. Secure the thread.

6. Make a second band, but sew through the 8° of the first band when making the top picot stitch **(e, f)**. Finish the band and secure the thread.

7. Cut a 3-ft. (1m) piece of beading thread. String a beading needle and place a bead stopper 6 in. (15cm) from the end. Sew through the first 8° on the top picot, pick up a dagger, a 15°, and a dagger, and sew through the next 8°. Pick up three long drop beads, and sew through the next 8°. Repeat this pattern between the top, bottom, and middle 8°s.

8. Cut 7 in. (18cm) of knitted wire and attach a flat-crimp end to each end. Weave the knitted wire between the Tilas and use jump rings to attach the crimp ends to the outer two holes of the slide clasp.

9. On each headpin, string a decorative bead and make a simple loop. Attach these dangles to the middle loops of the slide clasp to complete the bracelet.

TIP
If the hole of the decorative bead is too big for the headpin, use a 4mm crystal to prevent the headpin from going through.

Leviathan Luxe
Necklace

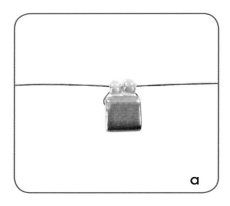

a

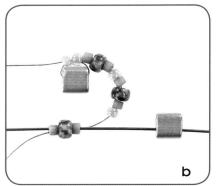

b

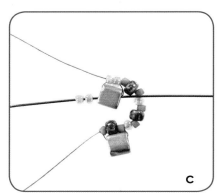

c

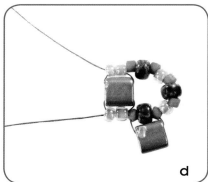

d

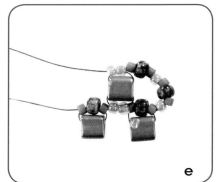

e

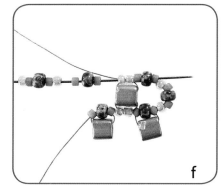

f

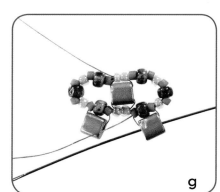

g

Two Beaded Necklace Ropes

1. Cut a 36-in. (91cm) piece of beading thread. Thread a beading needle and place a bead stopper 4 in. (10cm) from the end. Pick up two 11º seed beads and a cube bead and sew through the two 11ºs again **(a).**

2. Pick up a cylinder set (an 11º cylinder bead, a brown 8º seed bead, and a cylinder), an end-cylinder set (an 11º, a cylinder, a brown 8º, a cylinder, and an 11º), a cylinder set, and a cube, and sew through the last cylinder set **(b).**

3. Pick up two 11ºs and sew back through the previous cube **(c)**. Sew through the two 11ºs again **(d)**.

4. Pick up a cylinder set and a cube and sew through the cylinder set in the same direction **(e)**.

5. Pick up an end-cylinder set and a cylinder set. Sew through the top two 11ºs, the cylinder set, the end cylinder set, the cylinder set above the second cube sewn, and the cube **(f, g)**.

6. Pick up a cylinder set and sew through the cube and the new cylinder set **(h)**.

7. Pick up two 11ºs and a cube and sew through the new two 11ºs **(i)**. Pick up a cylinder set and sew in though the cube, then through the new cylinder set and repeat step 2–6 **(j)**. (Start by picking up an end-cylinder set **(k)**.) Secure the thread. Repeat steps 1–7 to make another necklace rope.

Note: You can flip the beadwork over to help relocate the stitching pattern.

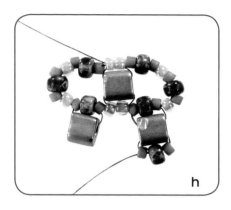

h

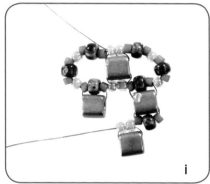

i

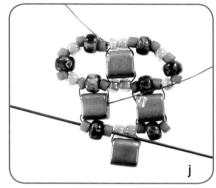

j

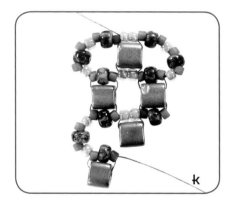

k

l

Materials
Necklace: 28 in. (71cm)
- **4** 12mm decorative beads
- **4** 8mm decorative beads
- 3g 4mm magatama beads, aqua-lined blue
- 4g 4mm cube beads, marbled metallic turquoise
- 4g 8° seed beads in each of **2** colors: copper and opaque brown blue picasso
- 3g 11° seed beads, transparent mint-lined
- 3g 11° cylinder beads, matte slate blue
- toggle clasp
- **2** triple-strand end caps
- **50** 8mm jump rings
- 36 in. (91cm) 20-gauge half-hard wire
- 5 ft. (1.2m) capture knitted wire, silver

Techniques
- Securing thread for separate ends (p. 13)
- Attaching end caps (p. 15)
- Making simple loops (p. 16)
- Making and attaching jump rings (p. 16)

Finishing

8. Cut a 14-in. (38cm), 16-in. (41cm), and 17-in. (43cm) piece of knitted wire. Stack the knitted wire as follows: Stack the shorter knitted wire as the inner strand, followed by the middle, and the longest at the other end. Attach an end cap over all three knitted wires on each end.

9. Cut a 1¾-in. (4.4cm) piece of half-hard wire and make a simple loop. String a decorative bead and make another simple loop. Repeat to make eight beaded links. Attach one small link between the bottom of the beaded necklace and the end cap. Attach a large link between the bottom of the beaded necklace rope and the end cap. Attach the rest of the links and the clasp to the top of the beaded necklace rope. On each jump ring, string a copper 8°, a magatama bead, and a copper 8°, and attach to a sewn cube. Repeat to complete the necklace **(l)**.

Through the Grape Vines

Earrings

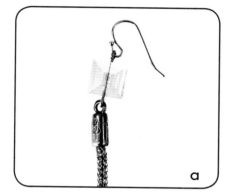

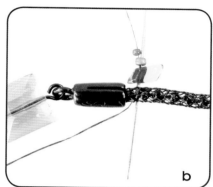

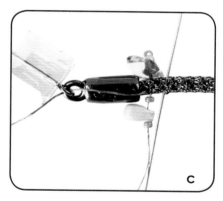

Earrings

1. Cut a 3-in. (7.6cm) piece of knitted wire. Attach an end cap to one end and a terminator to the other end. Cut 1¾ in. (4.4cm) of half-hard wire and make a simple loop on one end. String a decorative bead and make another simple loop. Attach an earring hook to one loop and the end cap to the other **(a)**.

2. Cut a 24-in. (61cm) piece of beading thread. Thread the beading needle and place a bead stopper 4 in. (10cm) from the end. Sew through the knitted wire close to the end cap, and pick up a magatama bead, an 11º seed bead, and a 15º seed bead. Sew back down through the 11º, the magatama, and the knitted wire. You have completed one picot stitch **(b)**.

3. Pick up a 15º, a drop, and a 15º, and sew up through the knitted wire to begin another picot stitch **(c)**. Alternate two picot stitches randomly on the knitted wire in all directions, leaving more space between the picot stitches at the bottom of the earring.

4. Secure the thread to finish. Make a second earring.

Materials

Earrings: 3 in. (7.6cm)

- **2** 10mm decorative beads
- 3g 4x7mm long magatama beads, light cranberry-lined topaz luster
- 3g 3.5mm long drop beads, matte yellow gold
- 2g 11º seed beads, matte yellow gold
- 2g 15º seed beads, dyed opaque pumpkin
- pair of earring hooks
- **2** single-strand end caps
- **2** short terminators
- 4 in. (10cm) 22-gauge half-hard wire
- 6 in. (15cm) capture knitted wire, olivine

Techniques

- Securing thread for stitched components (p. 14)
- Attaching end caps (p. 15)
- Attaching terminators (p. 15)
- Making simple loops (p. 16)

Suncatcher
Bracelet

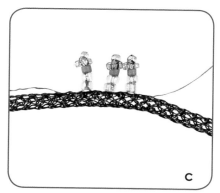

Bracelet

1. Cut a 24-in. (61cm) piece of beading thread. Thread a beading needle and place a bead stopper 4 in. (10cm) from the end. Start ½ in. (1cm) from the end of the knitted wire and sew through a knit-hole.

2. Pick up two 11º seed beads, a cylinder bead, and three 15º seed beads, and sew back through the cylinder, two 11ºs, and the next knit-hole up **(a, b)**. Repeat the picot stitch to the end of the knitted wire **(c)** and secure the thread.

Materials

Bracelet: 6½ in. (17cm)

- **15** 8mm faceted rondelle crystals
- **12** 6mm faceted rondelle crystals
- **12** 5mm faceted rondelle crystals
- 4g petal beads, matte dark teal AB
- 3g 11º seed beads, silver-lined gold AB
- 3g 11º cylinder beads, matte slate blue
- 3g 15º seed beads, transparent violet luster
- double-strand slide clasp
- **4** 4mm jump rings
- 18 in. (46cm) beading wire, 0.014, silver color
- 36 in. (91cm) hollow knitted wire, purple

Techniques

- Securing thread for separate ends (p. 13)
- Making folded crimps (p. 14)
- Making and attaching jump rings (p. 16)

TIP
A great way to expand on each design is to make separate accessories using the same technique. Pick a design and see if you can reinterpret the technique to make a necklace to go with a bracelet or a great pair of earrings!

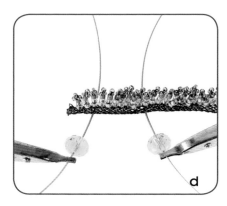
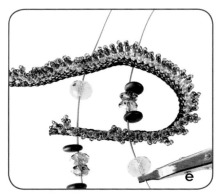

3. Cut two 9-in. (31cm) pieces of beading wire and place a bead stopper 3 in. (8cm) from the ends. String an 8mm bead on both wires, and with the beaded portion of the knitted wire facing up, pass the beading wire through an open knit-hole just below the beaded portion. Pass the second beading wire through a knit-hole 1 in. (2.5cm) from the first beading wire **(d)**.

4. On the left beading wire, string an 8mm bead. On the right beading wire, string a petal bead, a 6mm bead, a 5mm bead, and a petal. Loop the knitted wire around and pass the beading wire through the knit-holes again **(e)**.

5. Continue stringing, alternating the beads on the beading wire and making different sized loops with the beaded knitted wire. Once the beading wire is all strung, attach both loops of a clasp half to each end of the bracelet (use jump rings, if necessary).

Spanish
Sahara
Necklace

Materials

Necklace: 20 in. (51cm)

- **20** 40–60mm coral beads
- **6** 8–20mm decorative beads
- **36** 5mm brass faceted beads
- **36** 5mm brass disk beads
- **4g** 3mm cube beads, metallic bronze
- **3g** 2.5mm faceted round crystals, Siam
- **2g** 8º seed beads, matte metallic raspberry
- **1g** 11º cylinder beads, metallic bronze
- **3g** 11º seed beads in each of **2** colors: opaque red and transparent matte dark red
- toggle clasp
- **4** triple-strand end caps
- **2** 2mm crimp tubes
- **2** 4mm jump rings
- **4 in.** (10cm) 20-gauge half-hard wire
- **8 in.** (20cm) beading wire, 0.19, garnet
- **13 in.** (33cm) capture knitted wire in each of **3** colors: red, fall, and tan/gold

Techniques

- Securing thread for separate ends (p. 13)
- Making folded crimps (p. 14)
- Attaching end caps (p. 15)
- Making simple loops (p. 16)
- Making and attaching jump rings (p. 16)

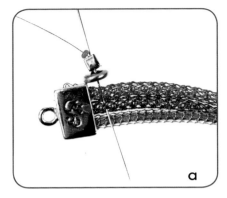

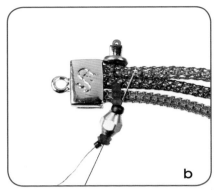

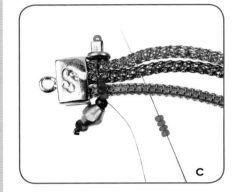

Necklace

1. Cut 6½-in. (16.5cm) pieces of all knitted wires. Stack the knitted wires in this order: red, fall, and tan. Attach the end caps to each end of all three wires.

2. Cut a 36-in. (91cm) piece of beading thread. Thread a beading needle and place a bead stopper 4 in. (10cm) from the end. With the leather knitted wire facing the bottom, sew up through the capture knitted wires close to the end cap and pick up a disk, a cube bead, and an opaque red 11º seed bead and sew back through the cube, the disk, and the capture knitted wires **(a)**.

3. Pick up four matte red 11º seed beads, an 8º seed bead, a brass bead, a crystal, and a cylinder bead, and sew back through the crystal, brass bead, and 8º **(b)**.

4. Pick up four matte red 11ºs, and sew behind the leather knitted wire, then through the capture knitted wire about ½ in. (1cm) from the last top picot stitch **(c)**. Repeat the top and bottom picot stitch to the end of the knitted wire and secure the thread. Make a second beaded rope. The faceted brass beads should point inside the necklace.

Note: Curve the stitched neck rope by gently sculpting and bending it with your fingers. The knitted wires should be stiff enough to bow a little bit.

5. Cut a 2-in. (5cm) piece of half-hard wire. Make a simple loop on one end, string two 8–20mm decorative beads, and make another simple loop. Attach the decorative bead link to an end cap, and attach half of a toggle clasp with a 4mm jump ring. Attach the other clasp half to the other beaded rope. On the beading wire, string the coral and decorative beads, and then crimp to the remaining end caps on each end of the beaded rope **(d)**.

Urban Envy
Earrings

Materials

Earrings: 4½ in. (6cm)

- **2** 12mm decorative beads
- **22** 5mm rondelle wood beads
- 2g 8º seed beads, gunmetal
- pair of earring hooks
- **2** triple-strand end caps
- 18 in. (46cm) jewelry chain, 2mm links
- 4 in. (10cm) 22-gauge half-hard wire
- 12 in. (30cm) capture knitted wire, pearlesque AB hematite

Techniques

- Securing thread for stitched components (p. 14)
- Attaching end caps (p. 15)
- Making simple loops (p. 16)

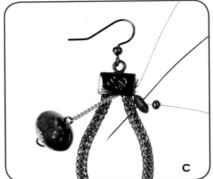

Earrings

1. Cut a 6-in. (15cm) piece of knitted wire, a ½-in. (1cm) piece of chain, and a 24-in. (61cm) piece of beading thread. Thread a beading needle and place a bead stopper 4 in. (10cm) from the end. Sew through the top of the knitted wire on each end, picking up the chain between them **(a)**.

2. Hold the needle and thread out of the way and attach the knitted wire, end cap, and earring hook together. Cut a 2-in. (5cm) piece of 22-gauge wire, make a simple loop on one end, string a 12mm decorative bead, and make a simple loop. Attach the decorative bead link to the free end of the chain **(b)**.

3. Sew through the knitted wire just below the end cap (make sure the thread exits outside the knitted wire loop). Pick up a wood bead and an 8º seed bead, and sew back through the wood bead and knitted wire **(c)**. You have completed one picot stitch.

4. Sew back through the knitted wire without any beads, but angle the needle so the thread exits next to the last picot stitch **(d)**.

5. Repeat the picot stitch to the end of the knitted wire and secure the thread. Cut the chain into two pieces, each in 3-in. (8cm), 2-in. (5cm), and 1½-in. (4cm) lengths. Attach them to the simple loop below the decorative bead to finish the earring.

6. Make a second earring.

Spikes
& Stones
Bracelet

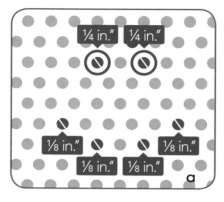

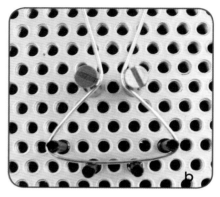

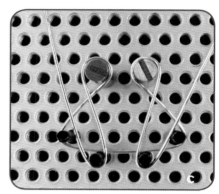

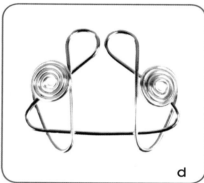

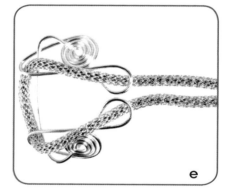

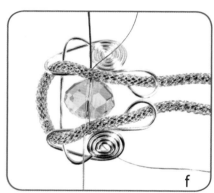

Bracelet

1. Attach the ¼-in. and ⅛-in. pegs on the jig as shown **(a)**.

2. Cut a 15-in. (38cm) piece of half-hard wire. Center the wire between the middle two pegs. Wrap the wire around the outside of those pegs and then bring the wire up next to the inside of the top two pegs **(b)**.

3. Wrap the wire ends around the outside of the top two pegs, then around the inside and then the outside of the bottom two pegs **(c)**. You have completed a wire component.

4. Remove the component from the jig. With each end, make a wire scroll that coils to the inside. Harden the wire component and then bring the wire scroll to the front of the component **(d)**. This will lock the component in place. Make a second component.

5. Cut a 6-in. (15cm) piece of knitted wire and go through the bottom loops of the component and over through the top loops as shown **(e)**. Gather the ends of the knitted wire and attach the end caps, jump rings, and clasp.

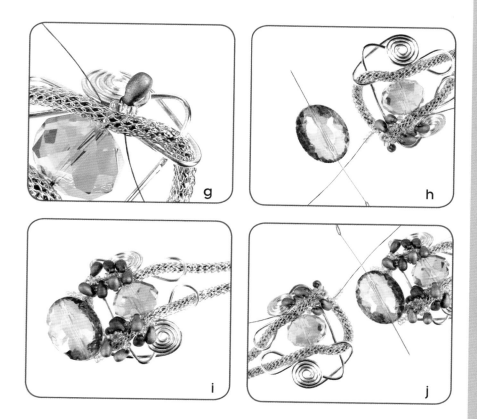

6. Cut a 24-in. (61cm) piece of beading thread. Thread a beading needle and place a bead stopper 4 in. (10cm) from the end. Starting between the two loops, sew through the knitted wire. Pick up a 12mm decorative bead and sew through the knitted wire on the other side. Sew back through the knitted wire and decorative bead **(f)**.

7. Pick up an 11º seed bead, a drop bead, and an 11º, and sew back though the knitted wire **(g)**. You have completed one picot stitch. Repeat the picot stitch randomly throughout the knitted wire between the decorative bead and where the knitted wire goes into the bottom of the wire component.

8. After the last picot stitch, pick up three 11ºs, a 35mm decorative bead, and three 11ºs, and sew through the other side of the knitted wire, repeating the picot stitches **(h, i)**. Secure the thread.

9. Repeat steps 1–8 to make the second beaded band, except sew through the 35mm decorative bead of the finished beaded band to connect them together and to complete the bracelet **(j)**.

Materials

Bracelet: 7 in. (18cm)

- 35mm decorative bead
- **2** 12mm decorative beads
- 3g 3x5.5mm drop beads, matte metallic khaki iris
- 2g 11º seed beads, transparent light topaz
- toggle clasp
- **2** double-strand end caps
- **2** 4mm jump rings
- 30 in. (76cm) 20-gauge half-hard wire
- 24 in. capture knitted wire, pearlesque AB urban
- Now that's a Jig!*
  2 ¼-in. (6mm) pegs
  4 ⅛-in. (3mm) pegs

You can substitute a WigJig or another peg-based tool for this project.

Techniques

- Securing thread for stitched components (p. 14)
- Attaching end caps (p. 15)
- Making and attaching jump rings (p. 16)
- Making wire scrolls (p. 17)
- Hardening half-hard wire (p. 17)

Aquarian
Necklace

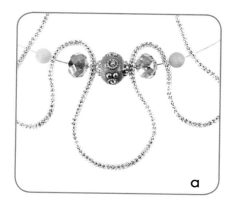 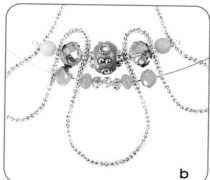

Necklace

1. Cut a 6-in. (15cm) piece of half-hard wire. Go through the center of the knitted wire, string a 20mm decorative bead, and go through a point 2½ in. (6cm) from the center of the piece of knitted wire (the decorative bead will sit between the knitted wire loop). String an 8–12mm decorative bead and go through a point 1 in. (2.5cm) from where the wire exited. String another 8–12mm decorative bead and go through a point 3½ in. (9cm) from where the wire exited. With the other end of the wire, repeat on the other side **(a)**.

Note: Adjusting the loops to be even on the wire can be tricky.
I used a straight pin to mark each measurement on the knitted wire.
Worked like magic!

2. Push the loops together and make a simple loop close to the knitted wire on each wire end.

3. Use the remaining wire to go through 4–7mm decorative beads and through the center loops just below the previous decorative beads. Make a simple loop close to the knitted wire on each wire end **(b)**.

Materials
Necklace: 20 in. (51cm)
- 20mm decorative bead
- **6** 8–12mm decorative beads
- **7** 4–7mm decorative bead
- 6g 3.5mm long drop beads, matte yellow gold
- 4g 8º seed beads, opaque chartreuse picasso
- 5g 11º seed beads, mint-lined aqua
- 5g 11º seed beads, bright copper
- toggle clasp
- **2** single-strand end caps
- **2** 4mm jump rings
- 12 in. (30cm) 22-gauge half-hard wire
- 36 in. (91cm) capture knitted wire, pearlesque silver AB

Techniques
- Securing thread for separate ends (p. 13)
- Attaching end caps (p. 15)
- Making and attaching jump rings (p. 16)

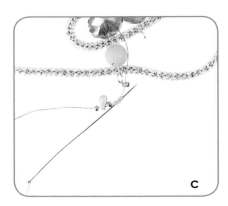

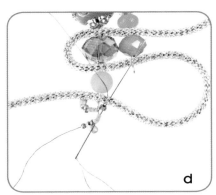

c

d

e

4. Cut an 18-in. (46cm) piece of beading thread. Thread a beading needle and place a bead stopper 4 in. (10cm) from the end. Start from the left-most loop just below the simple loop and sew down through the knitted wire. Pick up an 8° seed bead, three aqua 11° seed beads, a copper 11° seed bead, a drop, and a copper 11°, and sew back through the three aqua 11°s **(c)**.

5. Pick up another set of the same beads, and sew back through the three aqua 11°s, the 8°, and the knitted wire **(d)**. You have completed one picot stitch.

6. Pick up an 8° and a copper 11°, and sew back through the 8° and the knitted wire, but angle the needle to exit on the right side of the bottom picot stitch **(e)**. Continue stitching to cover three-quarters of the loop with picot stitches and then pick up a 4mm decorative bead. Sew through the middle knitted wire loop and continue making picot stitches to meet the last knitted wire loop.

7. Make picot stitches to the end of the loop and secure the threads. Taper the picot stitches 1 in. (2.5cm) above the simple loop by cutting a new piece of thread and reducing the number of beads used to make the picot stitch. (The last picot stitch should be an 8°, an aqua 11°, and a copper 11°.) Secure the threads. Attach the end caps, jump rings, and clasp to complete the necklace.

Rhapsody
Earrings

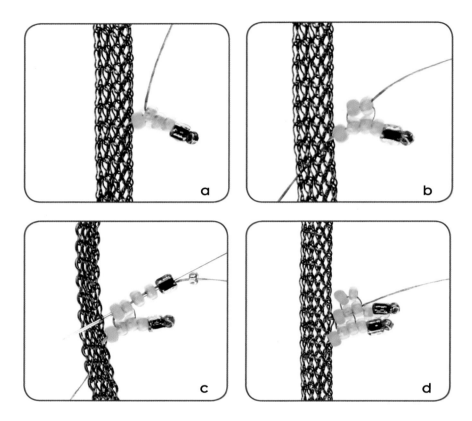

Earrings

1. Cut a 1¼-in. (3.2cm) piece of knitted wire and attach an end cap to each end. Use jump rings to attach an earring hook to one end and a decorative chain link to the other end. On a headpin, string a decorative bead and make a simple loop. Attach the loop to the decorative chain link.

2. Cut a 24-in. (61cm) piece of beading thread. Thread a beading needle and place a bead stopper 4 in. (10cm) from the end. Sew through the first knit-hole on the right side just above the flat end cap. Pick up a turquoise 11º seed bead, three aqua 11º seed beads, an 8º seed bead, and a 15º seed bead. Sew back through the 8º and three aqua 11ºs **(a)**. You have completed one picot stitch.

3. Pick up a turquoise and an aqua 11º and sew down through the two aqua 11ºs from the first picot stitch. Then sew back up through the turquoise and aqua 11º again **(b)**.

4. Pick up two aqua 11ºs, an 8º, and a 15º, and sew back through the 8º, three aqua 11ºs, the turquoise 11º, and the next knit-hole above the last stitch **(c)**.

5. Sew up through the turquoise 11º and two aqua 11ºs, pick up an aqua and a turquoise 11º, and sew up through the first two aqua 11ºs **(d)**.

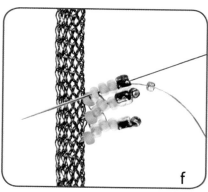

6. Sew down through the turquoise and aqua 11º and the next knit-hole up **(e)**.

7. Sew up through the turquoise and aqua 11º and pick up two aqua 11ºs, an 8º, and a 15º to make the next picot stitch **(f)**. Repeat the picot stitches to the end of the knitted wire to complete the earring.

8. Make a second earring.

Materials

Earrings: 2 in. (5cm)

- **2** 6mm decorative beads
- 1g 8º seed beads, emerald-lined blue luster
- 1g 11º seed beads in each of **2** colors: opaque turquoise and mint-lined aqua
- 1g 15º seed beads, silver-lined aqua
- **2** 8mm decorative jewelry chain links
- pair of earring hooks
- **4** flat-crimp ends
- **4** 3mm jump rings
- **2** 1-in (2.5cm) headpins
- 3½ in. (8.9cm) flat knitted wire, vintage bronze

Techniques

- Securing thread for stitched components (p. 14)
- Attaching flat crimp ends (p. 15)
- Making simple loops (p. 16)
- Making and attaching jump rings (p. 16)

Paris in the Rain
Bracelet

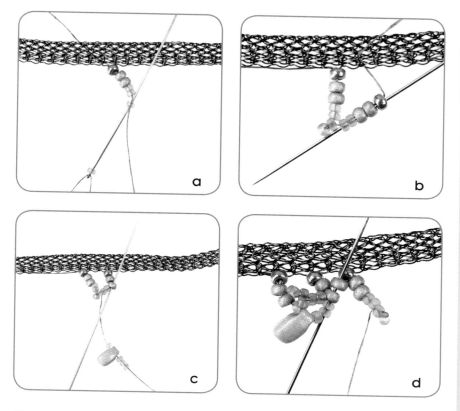

a

b

c

d

Beaded Bracelet Band

1. Cut a 24-in. (61cm) piece of beading thread. Thread the beading needle and place a bead stopper 4 in. (10cm) from the end. Starting on one end, sew through a knit-hole on the edge of the knitted wire. Pick up a copper 11º seed bead, two gold 11º seed beads, and four 15º seed beads, and sew back through the third 15º **(a)**.

2. Pick up two 15ºs, two gold 11ºs, and a copper 11º. Skip one knit-hole and sew through the next hole on the edge of the knitted wire **(b)**. You have completed one picot stitch. Sew back through the last 11º and 15º.

3. Pick up a 15º, a drop bead, and three 15ºs, and sew through the first gold 11º added in the last row of stitched beads **(c)**.

4. Pick up a gold 11º and a copper 11º. Skip a knit-hole and sew through the next. Sew back through the copper 11º and make another picot. Sew up through the two 15ºs and two gold 11ºs of the last stitched beads **(d)**.

Materials
Bracelet: 7 in. (18cm)
- **18** 4–15mm decorative beads
- 3g 3x5.5mm long drop bead matte gold
- 3g 11º seed beads, bright copper
- 2g 11º seed beads, matte yellow gold
- 2g 15º seed beads, matte transparent aqua
- toggle clasp
- **2** double-strand end caps
- **2** flat-crimp ends
- **2** 2mm crimp tubes
- **2** 6mm jump ring
- 12 in. (30cm) beading wire, .019, bronze
- 7 in. (18cm) flat knitted wire, vintage bronze
- 14 in (36cm) leather knitted wire, gold/tan

Techniques
- Securing thread for separate threads (p. 13)
- Making folded crimps (p. 14)
- Attaching end caps (p. 15)
- Attaching flat crimp ends (p. 15)
- Making simple loops (p. 16)

5. Sew through the two gold 11°s and two 15°s and add another drop bead as before **(e)**. Alternate the drop and non-drop picot stitches for the rest of the knitted wire length and secure the threads.

6. Cut a 24-in. (61cm) piece of beading thread. Thread the beading needle and place a bead stopper 4 in. (10cm) from the end. Pick up two copper 11°s and sew through a knit-hole on the top edge above the first picot stitch below **(f)**.

7. Sew through the two copper 11°s and pick up three copper 11°s **(g)**. Sew through the next knit-hole, and then sew back through the two new copper 11°s. Pick up three copper 11°s, and repeat the picot stitch for the rest of the knitted wire. Secure the threads and attach the flat crimp caps to finish the band.

Finishing

8. Cut two 7-in. (18cm) pieces of leather knitted wire. Gather the ends and attach the double-strand end caps to both ends. Attach the jump rings and toggle clasp to the end caps. Attach the flat end cap to the beaded bracelet band and then attach it to the jump rings.

9. String the decorative beads with the beading wire and crimp it to the jump rings to complete the bracelet.

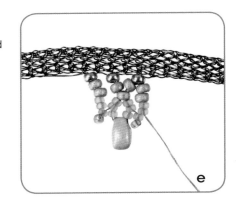

e

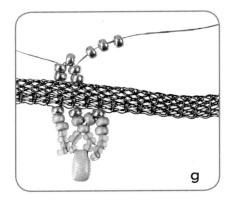

f

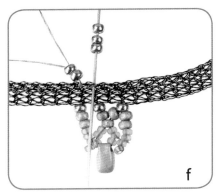

g

Graffiti
Earrings

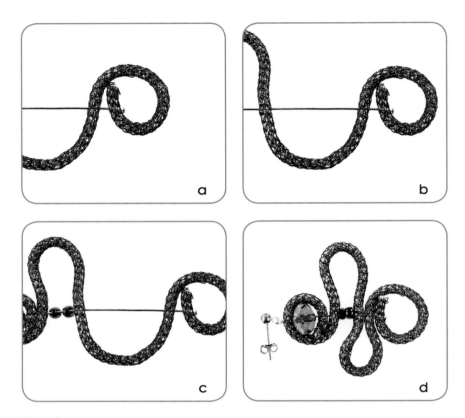

a

b

c

d

Earrings

1. Cut a 9-in. (23cm) piece of knitted wire, make a ½-in. (1.3cm) diameter coil at one end, and pass the headpin through the inside of the loop **(a)**.

2. Measure 1½ in. (4cm) from that point and pass the headpin through the knitted wire to make the second loop **(b)**.

3. String two drop beads and measure 2 in. (5cm) from that point. Pass the headpin through the knitted wire to make the third loop **(c)**.

4. Make a 1-in. (2.5cm) coil with the remaining knitted wire and pass the headpin through it, stringing one 8mm crystal rondelle (it will nest inside the coil). Push the knitted wire coils and loops together and make a simple loop close to the last coil. Attach an earring post **(d)**.

e

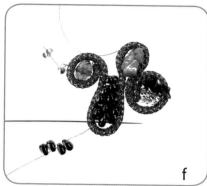

f

Materials

Earring size: 1½ in. (4cm)

- **2** 8mm faceted rondelle crystals
- **20** 4mm coral chips
- **14** 3mm bicone crystals
- **8** 3mm stone chips
- 3g 3x5.5 long drop beads, metallic iris AB
- pair of earring posts
- **2** 2-in. (5cm) headpins
- 18 in. (46cm) capture knitted wire, purple passion

Techniques

- Securing thread for separate ends (p. 13)
- Making simple loops (p. 16)

5. Cut a 36-in. (91cm) piece of beading thread. Thread a beading needle and place a bead stopper 4 in. (10cm) from the end. With the longest loop pointing down, start on the left side below the headpin and sew down through the bottom-most knitted wire coil. Pick up three 3mm crystals and sew through the bottom of the knitted wire loop. Sew back through the knitted wire, pick up four 3mm crystals, and sew up through the top of the knitted wire loop **(e)**.

6. Continue to sew back and fourth to "paint in" the loops with beads and go through the knitted wire to get to another loop. Use the coral beads on the bottom loop, the stone chips on the smaller right loop, and the drop beads for the large left loop, but graduate the number of drop beads used so they fill in the loop **(f)**. Secure the thread to complete the earring.

7. Make a second earring.

Mighty Rivers
Necklace

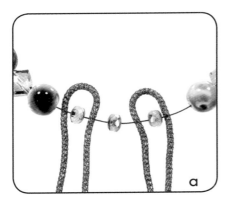

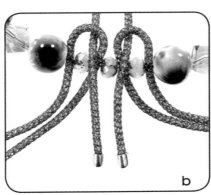

Necklace Rope

1. Cut a 17-in. (43cm), a 13-in. (33cm), and a 12-in. (30cm) piece of knitted wire and attach a terminator to each knitted wire end.

2. String half of the necklace rope on the beading wire: String an 8mm decorative bead, 13 8mm wood beads, two 10mm decorative beads, two wood beads, and five 12–30mm decorative beads.

3. Make a half-loop with the two smaller pieces of knitted wire. Pass the beading wire through the knitted wires, stringing a 6mm decorative bead between loop as shown **(a)**.

4. String the rest of the necklace with the matching decorative beads and wood beads. Crimp each end to a jump ring and attach the clasp. Pass the longer piece of knitted wire under and through the two knitted wire loops **(b)**.

Note: Stagger each knitted wire length so they graduate in size to be longer in the middle.

Materials
Necklace: 20 in. (51cm)

- **11** matching pairs of 8–30mm decorative beads
- **3** 15–20mm decorative beads
- **32** 8mm round wood beads
- **3** 6mm decorative beads
- **22** 4mm faceted rondelle crystals
- **50** 3mm faceted round crystals
- 3g 8º seed beads, transparent gray AB
- 1g 15º seed beads, matte sea foam
- toggle clasp
- **6** short terminators
- **2** 2mm crimp tubes
- **2** 1-in. (2.5cm) headpins
- **2** 4mm jump rings
- 24 in. (61cm) 22-gauge half-hard wire
- 36 in. (91cm) beading wire, dark blue lapis
- 3½ ft. (1m) capture knitted wire, fall

Techniques
- Securing thread for stitched components (p. 14)
- Making folded crimps (p. 14)
- Attaching terminators (p. 15)
- Making simple loops (p. 16)
- Making and attaching jump rings (p. 16)

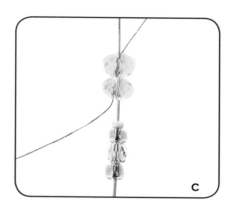

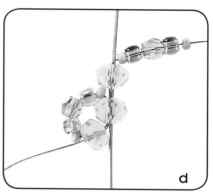

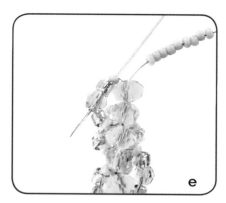

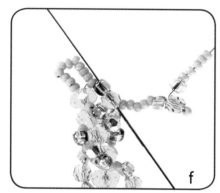

Beaded Spiral Pendant

5. Cut a 5-ft. (1.5m) piece of beading thread. Thread a beading needle and place a bead stopper 4 in. (10cm) from the end.

6. Pick up two 4mm crystals and one bead set (a 15º seed bead, an 8º seed bead, a 3mm crystal, an 8º, and a 15º), and sew up through the two 4mm crystals **(c)**.

7. Pick up a 4mm crystal and a bead set and sew up through the second and last 4mm crystal **(d)**. Repeat this stitch to sew twenty 4mm crystals together in a spiral rope.

8. Pick up ten 15ºs and sew down through the 15º, 8º, and 3mm crystal of the last bead set to make a bead loop at the top **(e)**. Make the additional embellished picot stitches by picking up five 15ºs, an 8º, a 3mm crystal, and a 15º. Sew up through the 3mm crystal, pick up an 8º and five 15ºs, and then sew up through the 3mm crystal and 8º of the bead set **(f)**.

9. Pick up a 15º, a 8º, and a 15º, and sew down through the 8º and 15º of the next bead set. Continue the picot stitch to the last bead set and secure the thread.

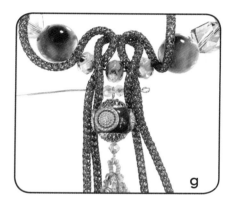

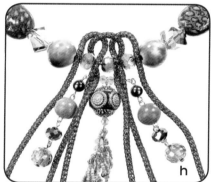

Finishing

10. Cut an 1¾-in. (4.4cm) piece of half-hard wire and make a simple loop on one end. String a 20mm decorative bead and make another simple loop.

11. Attach the beaded spiral pendant to a loop on the decorative bead link.

12. Cut a 2-in. (5cm) piece wire, make a simple loop on one end, and go through the right two knitted wires just below the 6mm decorative beads. String a 4mm crystal, the decorative bead link, and a 4mm crystal, and then go through the next two knitted wires **(g)**. Make a simple loop close to the knitted wire.

13. Repeat step 10 with the remaining wood beads and decorative beads and attach in a chain to the simple loops from step 12 **(h)**.

High Tide
Earrings

a

b

c

Materials

Earrings: 2½ in. (6cm)

- **2** 15mm faceted pear-shaped cabochons
- 4g (4–6mm) coral chips, angel skin
- 1g 11º seed beads, semi-frosted mint-lined aqua
- 1g 15º seed beads, matte dark aqua
- pair of earring hooks
- **2** double-strand end caps
- 8 in. (20cm) capture knitted wire, fall
- 3x3 in (8x8cm) suede fabric swatch
- tube of jewelers glue

Techniques

- Securing thread for stitched components (p. 14)
- Attaching end caps (p. 15)

Earrings

1. Glue a 15mm cabochon to the suede. Let the glue dry and trim the suede to 2mm around the stone **(a)**.

2. Cut a 4-in. (10cm) piece of knitted wire and attach an end cap. Attach the end cap to both ends of the knitted wire **(b)**. Attach an earring wire to the end cap. Pin the knitted wire to the suede edge around the stone. The end cap of the knitted wire should be aligned evenly at the top of the cabochon **(c)**.

TIP
Heard the phrase measure twice, cut once? I would recommend wrapping the knitted wire around the stone before attaching the end caps to get the perfect fit.

 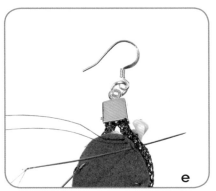

3. Cut a 24-in. (61cm) piece of beading thread. Thread a beading needle and place a bead stopper 4 in. (10cm) from the end. From the backside of the stone just below the end cap, sew up through the suede and knitted wire. Pick up two or three pieces of coral, an 11º seed bead, and a 15º seed bead. Sew back though the 11º, coral, knitted wire, and the suede **(d)**. You have completed one picot stitch.

4. Sew through the suede and knitted wire 2mm from the last picot stitch **(e)** and make another picot stitch. Continue to the end of the knitted wire. Secure the thread.

5. Make another earring.

Urban Design
Bracelet

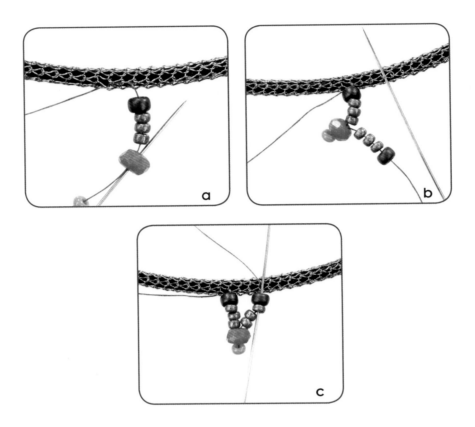

Bracelet

1. Attach an end cap to each end of the knitted wire. Attach a clasp half to each end cap with a 4mm jump ring.

2. Cut a 24-in. (61cm) piece of beading thread. Thread a beading needle and place a bead stopper 4 in. (10cm) from the end. Start 1 in. (2.5cm) from the end of the knitted wire and sew through a knit-hole. Pick up an 8º seed bead, three copper 11º seed beads, a crystal, and a coral 11º seed bead, and sew back through the crystal **(a)**.

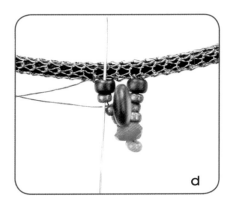

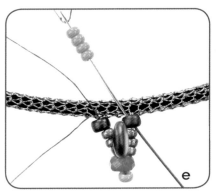

3. Pick up three copper 11°s and an 8°. Count three knit-holes and sew through the fourth one **(b)**.

4. Sew down through the 8° and the last copper 11° and pick up a petal bead. Sew up through the first copper 11° and 8° **(c, d)**.

5. Pick up four coral 11°s and sew down through the last 8° **(e)**. You have completed one picot stitch. Repeat the picot stitch seven more times and secure the thread.

6. Sew the beaded fringe in the middle of the knitted wire and at the other end of the knitted wire to complete the bracelet.

Materials

Bracelet: 23¹/₂ in. (60cm)

- **24** 3–4mm faceted rondelle crystals
- **24** petal beads, matte dark teal AB
- 3g 8° seed beads, matte metallic raspberry iris
- 3g 11° seed beads in each of **2** colors: coral and dark copper
- toggle clasp
- **2** single-strand end caps
- **2** 4mm jump rings
- 23 in. (60cm) leather knitted wire, copper/black

Techniques

- Securing thread for separate ends (p. 13)
- Attaching end caps (p. 15)
- Making and attaching jump rings (p. 16)

Blush
Earrings

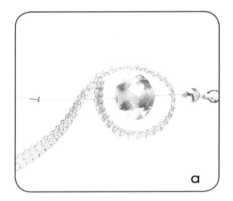

a

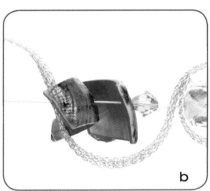

b

Earrings

1. Cut a 9-in. (2.5cm) piece of knitted wire and a 3½-in. (8.9cm) piece of beading wire. Attach a clamshell to one end of the beading wire. Pick up the knitted wire and make a loop that measures ¾ in. (2cm) in diameter, with ¼ in. (6mm) overlapping the inside. Pass the beading wire through the top. String a decorative bead and go through the bottom of the loop where the knitted wire overlaps **(a)**.

2. String a crimp tube, a 6mm crystal, two 15–20mm shell chips, and an 8mm pearl. Measure 1¼ in. (3cm) from the starting point on the knitted wire and go through it to make the second loop **(b)**.

Materials
Earrings: 4 in. (10cm)
- **8** 15–20mm coral chips
- **6** 15–20mm shell chips
- **2** 8mm decorative beads
- **2** 8mm button pearl beads
- **2** 6mm bicone crystals
- **4** 4mm decorative beads
- 2g 8º seed beads, silver-lined peach luster
- 2g 11º seed beads in each of **2** colors: dyed dark peach silver-lined alabaster and matte metallic dark copper
- 1g 15º seed beads, copper-lined opal
- pair of earring hooks
- **6** 2mm crimp tubes
- **2** clamshells
- 7 in. (18cm) beading wire, 0.019, bone
- 18 in. (10cm) flat knitted wire, rose gold

Techniques
- Securing thread for separate ends (p. 13)
- Making flattened crimps (p. 14)
- Attaching clamshells (p. 15)

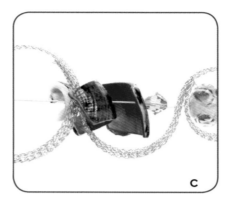

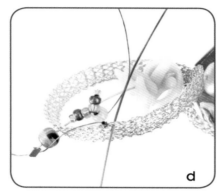

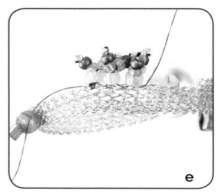

3. Coil the rest of the knitted wire to make a loop that measures 1¼ in. (3cm) in diameter. Go through the overlapping knitted wire and string a 15–20mm shell chip, a crimp tube, and four coral chips **(c)**.

4. Go through the bottom of the loop and string a 4mm decorative bead and a crimp tube. Crimp the end of the beading wire.

5. Crimp the first and second crimp tube to help hold the shape of the knitted wire. Cut a 24-in. (61cm) piece of beading thread. Thread a beading needle and place a bead stopper 4 in. (10cm) from the end. Sew through a knit-hole on the top edge, ½ in. (1cm) to the right of the last crimp tube. Pick up an 8º seed bead, a peach 11º seed bead, a copper 11º seed bead, and a 15º seed bead, and sew through the copper and peach 11º. Pick up a peach 11º, a copper 11º, and a 15º, and sew through the copper and peach 11º, the 8º, and the next knit-hole to the right **(d)**. You have completed one picot stitch.

6. Repeat this picot stitch to the top of the earring **(e)** and stop stitching about ½ in. (1cm) before the end. Secure the thread and attach an earring hook.

7. Make another earring.

Sunfire
Bracelet

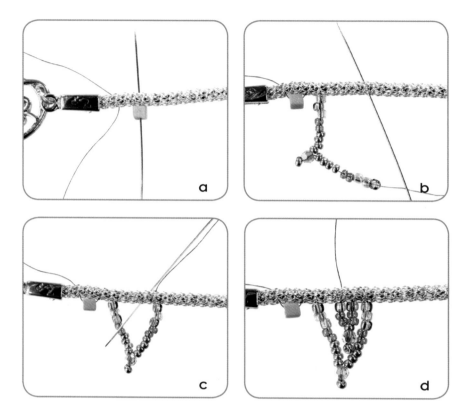

Bracelet

1. Attach an end cap to each end of the knitted wire. Attach a clasp half to each end cap with a 4mm jump ring.

2. Cut a 24-in. (61cm) piece of beading thread. Thread a beading needle and place a bead stopper 4 in. (10cm) from the end. Start near one end cap and sew down through the knitted wire. Pick up a cube bead, and sew up through the knitted wire **(a)**.

3. Sew back down through the knitted wire, but angle the needle to exit on the right side of the cube. Pick up three 8° seed beads, two raspberry 11° seed beads, four copper 11° seed beads, a 3mm round crystal, and a copper 11°. Sew back through the round crystal and pick up four copper 11°s, two raspberry 11°s, and three 8°s, and sew up through the knitted wire ½ in. (1cm) from the first 8° **(b)**. You have completed one picot stitch.

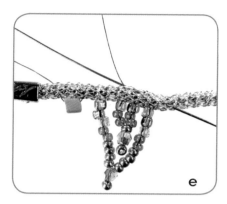

e

f

4. Sew down through the knitted wire, but angle the needle so the thread exits inside the picot stitch **(c)**. Make another picot stitch: Pick up an 8º, two raspberry 11ºs, a copper 11º, a round crystal, and a copper 11º. Sew back through the round crystal and copper 11º, pick up two raspberry 11ºs and a 8º, and then sew through the knitted wire **(d)**.

5. Sew down through the knitted wire, but angle the needle so the thread exits next to the picot stitch **(e)**. Alternate between cubes and picot stitches to the end of the knitted wire and secure the thread.

6. Make beaded wire flames: Cut a 3-in. (8cm) and a 1½-in. (4cm) piece of beading wire. With the longer wire, go through a cube. String one or two bicone crystals on each side of the wire and then crimp both ends together. Repeat on the same cube with the shorter beading wire **(f)**.

7. Make beaded wire flames on the rest of the cubes to complete the bracelet.

Materials

Bracelet: 7 in. (18cm)

- **28** 4mm bicone crystals
- **14** 3mm faceted round crystals
- **8** 3mm cube beads, matte sea foam
- 2g 8º seed beads, transparent gray AB
- 2g 11º seed beads in each of **2** colors: transparent raspberry luster and bright copper
- toggle clasp
- **2** single-strand end caps
- **16** crimp tubes
- **2** 4mm jump rings
- 36 in. (91cm) beading wire, 0.019, citrine
- 6½ in. (16.5cm) capture knitted wire, pearlesque silver AB

Techniques

- Securing thread for separate ends (p. 13)
- Making folded crimps (p. 14)
- Attaching end caps (p. 15)
- Making and attaching jump rings (p. 16)

Chrysalis
Earrings

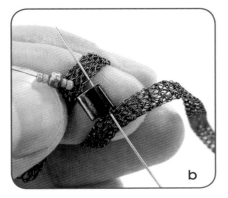

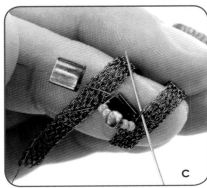

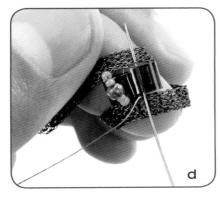

Earrings

1. Cut a 6-in. (15cm) piece of knitted wire and a 24-in. (61cm) piece of beading thread. Thread a beading needle and place a bead stopper 4 in. (10cm) from the end. Wrap the knitted wire around your index finger and sew through a knit-hole on the edge that's ½ in. (1cm) in from the end.

2. Pick up a Tila bead, and sew through a knit-hole on the top edge that is directly below the first knit-hole. Go back through the Tila and the first knit-hole again **(a)**.

3. Pick up two 15º seed beads, an 8º seed bead, and two 15ºs, and sew up through the knit-hole directly below the second hole in the Tila. Sew through the Tila and then the knit-hole directly above the second hole in the Tila **(b)**.

4. Pick up a Tila and sew through the knit-hole on the bottom knitted wire next to the Tila **(c)**. Repeat steps 2 and 3 **(d)** to stitch 15 Tilas together.

5. Trim the knitted wire close to the beadwork and attach a flat crimp end to each end. Attach the earring hook to a flat-crimp end with a 3mm jump ring.

6. String a 4mm bicone crystal on a headpin and make a simple loop. Using the remaining wire (that you trimmed), make a simple loop, string a rondelle crystal, and make a simple loop. Attach the rondelle crystal link to the flat crimp end and attach the 4mm crystal dangle to the rondelle crystal link.

7. Make another earring.

Materials

Earrings: 2 in. (5cm)

- **2** 6mm faceted rondelle crystals
- **2** 4mm bicone crystals
- **30** Tila beads, olive gold luster
- 1g 8º seed beads, opaque brown blue picasso
- 1g 15º seed beads, dyed opaque pumpkin
- pair of earring hooks
- **4** flat crimp ends
- **2** 2-in. (5cm) headpins
- **2** 3mm jump rings
- 12 in. (30cm) flat knitted wire, vintage bronze

Techniques

- Securing thread for separate ends (p. 13)
- Attaching flat crimp ends (p. 15)
- Making simple loops (p. 16)
- Making and attaching jump rings (p. 16)

Butterfly
Necklace

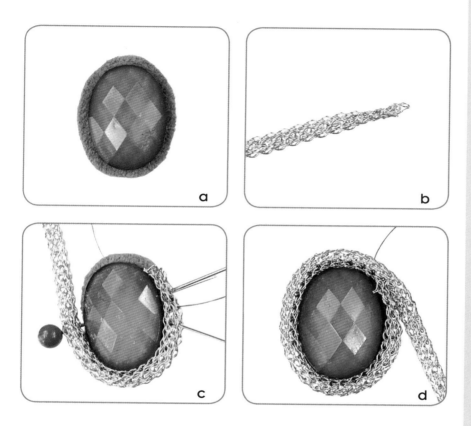

a

b

c

d

Necklace

1. Glue the stones to the suede. Let the glue dry and trim the suede to 2mm around the stone **(a)**.

2. Cut an 8-in. (20cm) piece of chartreuse knitted wire and push the knitted wire down to expose the capture chain. Trim three links and pull the knitted wire back over it. Press the end flat **(b)** and pin the knitted wire into a single coil around the suede edge of the 15mm stone **(c)**.

3. Cut a 24-in. (61cm) piece of beading thread. Thread a beading needle and place a bead stopper 4 in. (10cm) from the end. Starting from the back side of the stone, stitch through the suede and knitted wire all the way around to secure the first coil **(d)**.

Materials
Necklace: 18 in. (46cm)

- **4** 13x18mm faceted oval-shaped stones
- **4** 10x15mm faceted oval-shaped stones
- 5g 4mm cube beads, bright copper
- 5g 11º seed beads, silver-lined emerald AB
- 2g 11º cylinder beads, metallic brass
- 2g 15º seed beads, gold
- toggle clasp
- **4** double-strand end caps
- **2** 5mm jump rings
- 12 in. (30cm) 22-gauge half-hard wire
- 4¼ ft. (1.4m) capture knitted wire, chartreuse
- 24 in. (61cm) capture knitted wire, olivine
- 5x5 in. (8x8cm) suede fabric swatch
- tube of jewelers glue

Techniques

- Securing thread for stitched components (p. 14)
- Attaching end caps (p. 15)
- Making simple loops (p. 16)
- Making and attaching jump rings (p. 16)

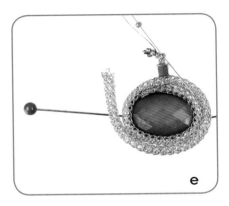

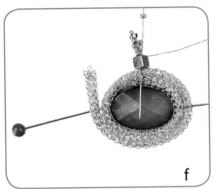

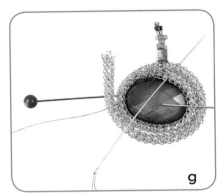

4. Trim the end of the capture chain, as in step 2. Coil and pin the rest of the knitted wire around the stone **(e)**. Sew up though both knitted wire coils, pick up a cube, four 11° seed beads, a cylinder bead, a 15° seed bead, and a cylinder, and sew back through the last 11° **(f)**. Pick up an 11° and sew down through the second 11°. Pick up an 11° and sew down through the cube and the knitted wire coils **(g)**. You have completed one picot stitch.

5. Sew up through the knitted wire coils, but angle the needle so the thread exits the next-to-last picot stitch. Repeat the picot stitch around the knitted wire coil and secure the thread. Set the beaded component aside and make seven more. With the smaller stones, use 6 in. (15cm) of olivine knitted wire.

6. Cut a 1½-in. (4cm) piece of half-hard wire and make a simple loop. Go through a cube on each of two beaded components and make another simple loop to connect the components. Repeat this step (use the photo on p. 104 as a guide) to attach the other components together.

7. Cut six 4½-in. (11cm) pieces of olivine knitted wire. Stack three pieces and attach an end cap to each end. Repeat with the three remaining pieces. Attach a toggle clasp half to one end of each three-strand link using jump rings. Repeat step 5 to connect the outer beaded components to the remaining two end caps.

Acknowledgments

First, I'd like to thank you for supporting my passion for design and the craft community. My goal is to help you learn some simple beading techniques, while experimenting with new materials and picking up some nifty tricks along the way. I hope this collection of designs and ideas will help inspire you to make your own fabulous designs.

Many thanks to my dear friends near and far for your support, love, and encouragement. You guys know who you are, and you inspire me to create every day.

Special thanks to my place of work for their humor, intrigue, and support. It's not easy trying to juggle several projects at a time, but you guys make it fun!

Very special thanks to my friends at *SilverSilk*: Nina, Nora, and John. Your friendship and support means the world to me. Many thanks to all my sponsors and special beading friends: Sara Oehler, Candie Cooper, Sarah Foxfurr, Brenda Schweder, Kenji Katsuoka, and Katie Hacker.

Many thanks to the Kalmbach team for making this book happen. Erica and Dianne, thanks for your support and answering any of my questions and teaching me new things along the way.

Thank you to my suppliers: *SilverSilk*, *Soft Flex Company*, *Jesse James Beads*, *Brenda Schweder Jewelry (Now That's a Jig!™)*, and *Miyuki Beads*.

Lastly, a very loving thanks to my family for their encouragement, opinions, discipline, and support.

About the author

Exploring should never be limited to any one area of creativity. Nealay exercises his craft in designing, educating and publishing his jewelry works. His first book, *Jewelry for the New Romantic: Unexpected Techniques with Beading Wire and Crystals*, explored the concept of integrating beading wire with bead weaving to create unique jewelry pieces with unusual textures—setting a milestone in his checklist of accomplishments. *Jewelry for the New Romantic* opened many new opportunities for Nealay, including regularly contributing to several beading magazines (nationally and internationally) and making television appearances on *Beads, Baubles, and Jewels* and *Jewel School* on the Jewelry Television network.

He has had the privilege to hold many instructional workshops at noted trade shows, such as Bead&Button and Bead Fest. Aside from his dedication to the publication industry, Nealay enjoys teaching, and even learning, from his local bead community in his hometown of Tulsa, Oklahoma.

Nealay's interest for the creative arts does not end at just jewelry. His passion for creating original works is used as a full-time art director for a noted design firm in the heart of Tulsa's booming arts district. Visit nealaypatel.com for more information or view Nealay's Pinterest page, Pinterest.com/nealaypatel.

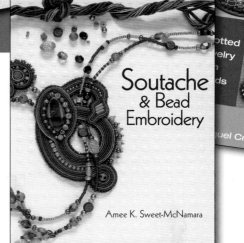